In Nomine Patris et Filii et Spiri.

Protestation

In all that I shall say in this book I submit to what is taught by Our mother, the Holy Roman Church; if there is anything in it contrary to this, it will be without my knowledge. Therefore, for the love of Our Lord, I beg the learned men who are to read it to look at it very carefully and to make known to me any faults of this nature which there may be in it and the many others which it will have of other kinds.

If there is anything good in it, let this be to the glory and honor of God in the service of His most sacred Mother, our Patroness and Lady.

Matthew R. Plese

The Definitive Guide
to Catholic Fasting & Abstinence

Matthew Plese

2nd Edition

THE DEFINITIVE GUIDE TO CATHOLIC FASTING AND ABSTINENCE

Matthew R. Plese

SECOND EDITION

© Our Lady of Victory Press, MMXXIV

ISBN 979-8-9877607-6-5

2ND PRINTING: JULY 2024

Our Lady of Victory Press is an imprint of The Meaning of Catholic, a lay apostolate dedicated to uniting Catholics against the enemies of Holy Church.

MeaningofCatholic.com

Design and layout by W. Flanders.

Our Lady of Victory, pray for us!

Medical disclaimer: Any suggestions taken based on this book should first be cleared by a competent and licensed medical personnel, if necessary and appropriate.

First edition printed by Our Lady of Victory Press on Candlemas, 2023.

TABLE OF CONTENTS

Preface to the Second Edition

In early 2023, I launched *The Definitive Guide to Fasting and Abstinence* based on over three years of research into the forgotten and untold history of how the Catholic Church went from roughly one-third of the year of fasting (and two-thirds as days of abstinence) to only two days of fasting. I published the book so that it would be available in time for Lent, and even though many priests said that 95% of it was new to them, I still had more research to undertake to finish my study of this forgotten history.

After another year of work, I'm delighted to launch the 2nd edition of the book. This edition features the following topics which were not covered (or covered only briefly) in the first edition: detailed explanations of how fasting changed in other countries besides America, including Spain and the Philippines, a detailed explanation of who was exempt from fasting and/or abstinence and how those changes were documented and taught in various catechisms over the centuries. I also cover Easter Week food traditions, highlighting their connection with the Lenten fast, Armenian fasting and abstinence rigors, Maronite fasting guidelines, the heroic example of St. John of the Cross and the Primitive Rule of Pope Innocent IV vs. the mitigated rule approved by Pope Eugenius IV, how the time of the meal on fasting days differed (e.g., sunset for Ember Days but 3 PM for the weekly devotional fasts), and so much more. Also included is practical advice on how to ease into and out of fasting.

Matthew Plese

Foreword to the First Edition

I am pleased to be able to write this preface for what seems to be and what is a work of art, a work of love. Fasting, a great means of self-mastery and love of God, cannot be reduced in its importance for the spiritual life though many have tried to sever this connection by abrogating the requirement to fast either in part or in whole. Its history is like a romance where at first it leads you into friendship and then into zealous love. However, not all romances have a happy ending or at least not all maintain that zeal which at first was on fire. This is also the case for fasting's history. While at first fasting was practiced with a zeal unheard of today, it was later lessened or abrogated. Sometimes it was truly a matter of mercy or of charity. Oftentimes, however, the reduction of fasting by the Church was a matter of pure acquiescence. It does not follow then that just because the Church requires you nowadays to fast twice a year that you should only fast twice a year or that it is okay to do so. It would not be the first case of imprudence on the part of the bishops to allow such a thing to develop.

If we are Catholic, truly Catholic, and love the Church, love Jesus Christ, and want to save our souls there will then be either implicitly or explicitly a desire for us to do everything we can to live in the fullest measure possible. However, this comes at a cost. It requires of us a great deal of work well beyond the minimum. Part of that cost is enduring the difficult fasts of antiquity. Part of that cost lies in research and studying. Here we have done that part for you. Living in the fullest measure possible in this regard is learning what is organic development regarding fasting and what is the fullness of fasting. The only way one is going to be able to know these things is if he learns fasting's forgotten and untold history. This book is that story.

Studying the history of fasting is only the first part. From there we must pray. We must pray to God that He gives us a love for fasting that through it we may give our hearts and our bodies entirely to Him. We must pray for courage and temperance and when we fast, we must seek the will of God through it, since if we do not, we risk loving ourselves more than we love God.

Knowing the history of fasting is only that first step as the work to be done is great and it is hard. It is hard work to fast like Pope St. Leo the Great. It is hard work to fast like St. John Chrysostom. However hard it may be, it is worth it, and it is a great joy, for in fasting heartily God gives us new flesh and a new heart. He takes away the stone and the rot. He gives us a clean heart. Don't neglect Him another day. Don't miss out on the opportunity to love Him more, and most importantly keep to the fullness of the Faith, to the fullness of tradition, for it is there that the love of God is on fire for men.

Tyler Gonzalez

Priestly Testimonials

"This work is highly important for faithful Catholics! Matthew has written a book that contains the potential for notable impact on our Prayer Life, Personal Sanctity, and increased historical understanding of the teachings of Holy Mother Church. Since Vatican II the understanding of Fasting, Holy Days of Obligation, and the need to gain self-control have been lessened by transfers of Solemnities and the emotional dispensations from fasting given by ecclesiastical authorities. Armed with this renewed knowledge of age-old practices used by serious Catholics in offering personal acts of sacrifice through abstinence and fasting, a barrier of a hum-drum prayer life can be broken, and Catholics can achieve new levels of Active Participation in the life of the Church." (Father Scott DuVall)

"To paraphrase St. John Henry Newman, prayer and fasting are the two wings that carry us to Heaven. We cannot achieve eternal life unless both wings are functioning. *The Definitive Guide to Catholic Fasting and Abstinence* is not only a history of the practice of fasting, but also more importantly a guide to show Catholics how to love fasting in an age where satisfaction for sin is most needed!" (Father John Lovell, Co-Founder of the Coalition for Canceled Priests)

"*The Definitive Guide to Catholic Fasting and Abstinence* fills a great lacuna in the life of the Church. Matthew's articulate and cogent account of an integral Catholic way of life is one which gives rightful place to the body and its healthy, holistic, and holy subordination to the soul and spirit. Matthew's book is not only a call to arms, but a call to the recovery of the vital narrative memories of the saints of yesterday, who in their fundamental anthropology, struggles, and strivings are no different from us, the saints of today. With sobriety, intelligence, and authentic piety, *The Definitive Guide to*

Catholic Fasting and Abstinence serves as a point of reference, understanding, and motivation so that the strength and the joy of our forefathers may be ours in the here and now." (Father Cassian DiRocco)

"Many ask what do I do to stem the tide of evil and promote the salvation of souls? This book gives us one of the most important tools. By giving a thorough history and explanation of the laws and practices of fasting and abstinence, the reader cannot help but be motivated to more than the current minimal requirements. The famous quote by Archbishop Fulton Sheen came to mind as I realized the potential for others to be moved by this book: 'Who will save the Church? ...the laity.' I believe a return to the Church's rich traditions could be a big part of the work of the laity to save the Church. This book will also inspire priests, as most of us were never instructed in this tradition but will be inspired as well to do more fasting and lead the souls in their care to use the power of fasting and abstinence." (Father Joseph Nicolosi).

The Rise of Catholic Fasting: Pre-Renaissance

Fasting in Biblical Times

In principio, in the beginning, the very first Commandment of God[1] to Adam and Eve was one of fasting from the fruit of the tree of the knowledge of good and evil (cf. Genesis 2:16-17), and their failure to fast brought sin and disorder to all of creation. The second sin of mankind was gluttony. Both are intricately tied to "the divine law of fasting and temperance" as St. Basil the Great teaches.

Both Elijah and Moses fasted for forty days in the Old Testament before seeing God. Until the Great Flood, man abstained entirely from the flesh meat of animals (cf. Genesis

9:2-3). Likewise, in the New Testament, St. John the Baptist, the greatest prophet (cf. Luke 7:28) fasted and his followers were characterized by their fasting. And our Blessed Lord also fasted for forty days (cf. Matthew 4:1-11) not for His own needs but to serve as an example for us. Our Redeemer said, "Unless you shall do penance, you shall all likewise perish" (Luke 13:3). Fasting and abstinence from certain foods has characterized the lives of mankind since the foundation of the world.

The Purpose of Fasting

The Church has hallowed the practice of fasting, encourages it, and mandates it at certain times. Why? The Angelic Doctor writes that fasting is practiced for a threefold purpose:

> First, in order to bridle the lusts of the flesh... Secondly, we have recourse to fasting in order that the mind may arise more freely to the contemplation of heavenly things: hence it is related of Daniel that he received a revelation from God after fasting for three weeks. Thirdly, in order to satisfy for sins: wherefore it is written: 'Be converted to Me with all your heart, in fasting and in weeping and in mourning.' The same is declared by Augustine in a sermon: 'Fasting cleanses the soul, raises the mind, subjects one's flesh to the spirit, renders the heart contrite and humble, scatters the clouds of concupiscence, quenches the fire of lust, kindles the true light of chastity.'[2]

St. Basil the Great also affirmed the importance of fasting for protection against demonic forces: "The fast is the weapon of protection against demons. Our Guardian Angels more readily stay with those who have cleansed our souls through fasting."

The Baltimore Catechism echoes these sentiments: "The Church commands us to fast and abstain, in order that we may mortify our passions and satisfy for our sins" (Baltimore Catechism #2 Q. 395). Concerning this rationale, Fr. Thomas Kinkead in *An Explanation of The Baltimore Catechism of Christian Doctrine* published in 1891 writes, "Remember it is our bodies that generally lead us into sin; if therefore we punish the body by fasting and mortification, we atone for the sin, and thus God wipes out a part of the temporal punishment due to it."

Pope St. Leo the Great in 461 wisely counseled that fasting is a means and not an end in itself. For those who could not observe the strictness of fasting, he sensibly said, "What we forego by fasting is to be given as alms to the poor."[3] To simply forgo fasting completely, even when for legitimate health reasons, does not excuse a person from the universal command to do penance (cf. Luke 13:3). It must be stated that we do not gain merits in the performance of penance, no matter how severe, if we are in the state of mortal sin. Staying in the state of grace is essential for meriting.

To Love Fasting

The Rule of St. Benedict written in 516 AD by the illustrious St. Benedict states in part: "O Lord, I place myself in your hands and dedicate myself to you. I pledge myself to do your will in all things: To love the Lord God with all my heart, all my soul, all my strength. Not to kill. Not to steal... To chastise the body. Not to seek after pleasures. To love fasting..."

How can we love fasting? Fr. Adalbert de Vogue, OSB explains, "To love fasting one must experience it, but to experience it one must love it. The way to get out of this circle is easy: trust in the word of God, in the example of the saints, in the great voice of tradition, and trusting in this witness, try it."[4]

To love fasting is our goal. Fasting should never be performed without an increase in prayer or almsgiving. It should not be performed grudgingly and in anger. Likewise, it should not be performed for the vain purpose of losing weight or even for the natural good of improving one's health. Fasting must have God as its end.

Purpose of Studying Fasting & Abstinence

Fasting is one of the chief means of penance we can perform to make satisfaction for sin, as our Lady of Fatima repeatedly requested. Understanding the decline of fasting over time in the Church should inspire us to observe these older customs and to encourage other Catholics to do so for the purpose of making satisfaction for sin.

The history of fasting in the Catholic Church, like other disciplines, has undergone considerable changes throughout the centuries. Unlike dogma, which is unchangeable, disciplines like fasting may change over time. However, in a modern Church that legislates fasting only two days a year, we find a woefully lacking answer to Heaven's incessant calls for penance and reparation.

While the purpose of fasting has remained the same, how fasting is observed has changed. As more Catholics seek to rediscover the traditions of earlier centuries and piously observe these traditions, they are often confused by the changing disciplines and exceptions for certain times, places, and circumstances. St. Francis de Sales remarked, "If you're able to fast, you will do well to observe some days beyond what are ordered by the Church."

This book will explain fasting and how it has changed over the centuries in one of the most complete compilations yet written. Unfortunately, most summaries of fasting are either inaccurate or woefully incomplete. However, rather than being a mere academic exercise, the purpose of studying the history of fasting is ultimately to help us rediscover these more ancient practices to better observe our Lord and our Blessed Mother's call for penance and reparation for sins.

Fasting in the Early Church Through the 5th Century

And the disciples of John and the Pharisees used to fast; and they come and say to him: Why do the disciples of John and of the Pharisees fast; but thy disciples do not fast? And Jesus saith to them: Can the children of the marriage fast, as long as the bridegroom is with them? As long as they have the bridegroom with them, they cannot fast. But the days will come when the bridegroom shall be taken away from them; and then they shall fast in those days (Mark 2:18-20).

Fasting has been a part of the Catholic Church since the time of the Apostles who instituted fasting shortly after our Redeemer's Ascension into Heaven. Fasting in the Apostolic Age consisted of two primary \ periods: the weekly devotional fasts and the Lenten Fast. This replaced the previous six Jewish fast days of Yom Kippur, Tisha B'Av, the Fast of Gedaliah, the Tenth of Tevet, the Seventeenth of Tammuz, and the Fast of Esther. Historically, Reform Jews only observed the Yom Kippur fast while Orthodox Jews observed all six fasts in addition to the voluntary weekly fasts of Thursday and Monday. Regarding the fast of Yom Kippur, the Catechism of Perseverance notes its importance:

> The Jews had one day of general fast; this was the festival of expiations. It was on this day only that the high priest entered the Holy of Holies. One he-goat was sacrificed, and another, after being loaded with the curse of all the sins of the people, was driven into the desert; it was called the scapegoat, or emissary goat. It represented our Lord loaded with the

sins of the world and led out of Jerusalem to be put to death. There were also extraordinary days of fasting in times of public calamity or particular affliction.[5]

Weekly Fasting

In the Early Church, fasting, which always included abstinence as part of it, was widely observed each week on Wednesday and Friday. This practice is still kept by some pious Catholics and Eastern Catholics. By contrast, the traditional days for Jewish fasting were Thursday and Monday on account of the Tradition that Moses went up Mount Sinai on Thursday and returned on a Monday, as mentioned in the Jewish midrash commenting on Exodus 19:24.

The *Didache*, the Teaching of the Apostles, written by the end of the first century states in chapter 8: "But let not your fasts be with the hypocrites; for they fast on the second and fifth day of the week; but fast on the fourth day and the Preparation." Since Sunday is the first day of the week, the fourth day referred to Wednesday and the day of Preparation referred to Friday. The phrase "day of preparation" preceding the sabbath on Saturday occurs in the Scriptures in Matthew 27:62; Mark 15:42; Luke 23:54; and John 19:14,31,42. All such instances unequivocally confirm that it refers to Friday.

On the rationale for fasting on these days, St. Peter of Alexandria, Patriarch of Alexandria until his death in 311 AD, explains: "On Wednesday because on this day the council of the Jews was gathered to betray our Lord; on Friday because on this day He suffered death for our salvation." Likewise, the 1875 Catechism of Father Michael Müller adds: "This practice began with Christianity itself, as we learn from St. Epiphanius, who says: 'It is ordained, by the law of the Apostles, to fast two days of the week.'"[6]

Rev. Hugo Hoever notes that Wednesday and Friday fasting became obligatory throughout the Diocese of Tours in the mid-400s by the decree of St. Perpetuus, Bishop of Tours, although they were previously obligatory by reason of custom:

> [St. Perpetuus] prescribed the manner of celebrating vigils in the different churches of the city, ordained that Wednesdays and Fridays should be fasts of precept, with the exception of certain times of the year.[7]

Some places added Saturday fasting as well, as noted by St. Francis de Sales who writes, "The early Christians selected Wednesday, Friday and Saturday as days of abstinence."[8]

Saturday fasting eventually became extended to the entire Church in the early 400s by Pope Innocent I who wrote: "Reason shows most clearly that we should fast on Saturday, because it stood between the sadness [of Good Friday] and the joy [of Easter Sunday]."[9] The Douay Catechism, written in 1649, in Question 554 explains the rationale for Saturday abstinence, which was then still universally practiced, even though the weekly fast on Saturday had long ended by that time: "To prepare ourselves for a devout keeping of the Sunday, as also in honor of the blessed Virgin Mary, who stood firm in the faith on that day, the apostles themselves wavering."[10]

The Apostolic Origin of the Lenten Fast

The great liturgist Dom Guéranger writes that the fast which precedes Easter originated with the Apostles themselves:

> The forty days' fast, which we call Lent, is the Church's preparation for Easter, and was instituted at the very commencement of Christianity. Our Blessed Lord Himself

sanctioned it by fasting forty days and forty nights in the desert; and though He would not impose it on the world by an express commandment (which, in that case, could not have been open to the power of dispensation), yet He showed plainly enough, by His own example, that fasting, which God had so frequently ordered in the old Law, was to be also practiced by the children of the new...The apostles, therefore, legislated for our weakness, by instituting, at the very commencement of the Christian Church, that the solemnity of Easter should be preceded by a universal fast.[11]

The *Catechism of the Liturgy by a Religious of the Sacred Heart* published by The Paulist Press, New York, 1919[12] affirms the apostolic origin of the Lenten fast: "The Lenten fast dates back to Apostolic times as is attested by Saint Jerome, Saint Leo the Great, Saint Cyril of Alexandria and others." In the 2nd century, St. Irenaeus wrote to Pope St. Victor I inquiring on how Easter should be celebrated, while mentioning the practice of fasting leading up to Easter.

Initially the Lenten fast was practiced by catechumens preparing for Baptism[13] with a universal fast for all the faithful observed only during Holy Week, in addition to the weekly fasts that were devotionally practiced. But early on, the baptized Christians began to join the catechumens in fasting on the days immediately preceding Easter. The duration of the fast varied with some churches observing one day, others several days, and yet others observing an intensive forty hour fast, in honor of the forty hours that the Lord spent in the sepulcher. By the third and fourth centuries, the fast became forty days in most places. St. Athanasius, in 339 AD, referred to the Lenten fast as a forty day fast that "the whole world" observed.[14]

Dr. K.A. Heinrich Kellner states the following regarding the Lenten fast in the ancient Church, noting the strictness that intensified in Holy Week and even more so on Good Friday and Holy Saturday:

> Among Catholics also abstinence was pushed to great lengths. The canons of Hippolytus prescribe for Holy Week only bread and salt. The Apostolic Constitutions will only permit bread, vegetables, salt, and water, in Lent, flesh and wine being forbidden; and, on the last two days of Holy Week, nothing whatsoever is to be eaten. The ascetics, whose acquaintance the Gallic pilgrim made in Jerusalem, never touched bread in Lent, but lived on flour and water. Only a few could keep so strict a fast, and generally speaking people were satisfied with abstaining from flesh and wine. But this lasted throughout the entire Lent, and Chrysostom tells us that in Antioch no flesh was eaten during the whole of Lent. Abstinence from milk and eggs (the so-called lacticinia) was also the general rule.[15]

Shortly after the legalization of Christianity in the Roman Empire, the bishops at the Council of Nicaea in 325 AD fixed the date of Easter as the first Sunday after the first full moon after the vernal equinox. The canons emerging from that council also referenced a forty-day Lenten season of fasting.

The Lenten fast was not merely a devotional fast but one of precept under penalty of sin. Father Stephen Keenan's Catechism from 1846 quotes St. Augustine (who lived from 354 – 430 AD) as saying: "Our fast at any other time is voluntary; but during Lent, we sin if we do not fast."[16]

One Meal A Day After Sunset

To the Early Christians, fasting was performed until sundown, in imitation of the previous Jewish tradition. Dom Guéranger's writings affirm, "It was the custom with the Jews, in the Old Law, not to take the one meal, allowed on fasting days, till sunset. The Christian Church adopted the same custom. It was scrupulously practiced, for many centuries, even in our Western countries. But, about the 9th century, some relaxation began to be introduced in the Latin Church."[17]

And notably in the early Church, fasting also included abstinence from wine, taking man back to the same diet that he practiced before God permitted Noah to eat meat and drink wine. As such, in apostolic times, the main meal was a small one, mainly of bread and vegetables. Fish, but not shellfish, became permitted on days of abstinence around the beginning of the 7th century.[18] The allowance of shellfish became permitted around the 10th century.[19] Hence, some Eastern Rite Catholics, in addition to Eastern Orthodox Christians, will abstain from meat, animal products, wine, oil, and fish on fasting days which harkens back to these ancient times. In fact, in Eastern Orthodoxy and in Eastern Rite Catholicism different fasting periods have different regulations with some permitting fish or oil and others forbidding them.[20] Great Lent is the strictest fasting period of the year for all Christians.

Remarkably, even water was forbidden during fasting times in the very ancient church. Fr. Alban Butler in *Moveable Feasts and Fasts* provides testimony of this when he writes:

> St. Fructuosus, the holy bishop of Tarragon in Spain, in the persecution of Valerian in 259, being led to martyrdom on a Friday at ten o'clock in the morning, refused to drink, because it was not the hour to break the fast of the day, though fatigued with imprisonment,

and standing in need of strength to sustain the conflict of his last agony. 'It is a fast,' said he: 'I refuse to drink; it is not yet the ninth hour; death itself shall not oblige me to abridge my fast.'[21]

The Pulpit Orator published in 1884 by Fr. Pustet & Company[22] similarly notes: "That we take only one full meal, Sundays excepted. The Christians of the first ages observed this ecclesiastical ordinance very exactly, after the setting of the sun. Nor did they drink water unless there was a necessity. A council at Aix-la-Chapelle declares: 'Only when necessity requires it, on account of hard labor or weakness, is it allowed to drink.'"

Prudentius, a Christian poet of the 4th century wrote about the fasting of St. Fructuosus in his Peristephanon.[23] Prudentius wrote, "Certain ones from the crowd a cup presented for the bishop to quaff but he refused it, saying 'I will not drink for we are fasting the ninth hour has not freed us from this duty.'"

This concept of having no water outside the meal and the meal being after 3pm on most fast days is defended by Tertullian.[24] And contrary to what some historians may suggest, the historicity and veracity of the account of St. Fructuosus is mentioned by St. Augustine and the Catholic Encyclopedia.[25] And, as far as the veracity of the hymn of Prudentius, this hymn is used in the Mozarabic Breviary for Matins and Lauds on his feast day.[26]

The Strictness of Holy Week

The Passion Fast is a term which refers to the fast which began for some as early as sunset on Holy Thursday and as late as 8 AM on Good Friday. No one was allowed to eat any food during that time until sunset on Holy Saturday, which – since most fasted for Communion – extended until the morning on

Easter Sunday. It was often called a "40 Hours Fast" and represents the original Lenten fast. For those who were too weak to follow this fast the minimum fast at this time was that of xerophagiae.

Xerophagiae is a diet of simple, dry, uncooked food, such as raw nuts, bread, fruits, and vegetables. Fish and oil are not part of it and neither are flesh nor animal products. It was a precept to fast on these only during Holy Week by custom and/or decree until approximately the time of Pope St. Gregory the Great (reigned 590 – 604 AD), who mentions nothing of it. It may still have been a custom at that time but no mention of it is made in the Decretals of Gregory IX published in 1234.

Fasting in the Life of Public Penitents

Those who have studied the history of the Roman Rite will recall that in ancient times public sinners were expelled from the Church on Ash Wednesday and received again on Holy Thursday. Whereas today we are more familiar with the journey that catechumens are making to receive the Sacraments of Initiation at the Easter Vigil, centuries ago, the penitents were also making a similar journey to the holiest of all celebrations: Easter. The Lenten fast was kept with rigor and keen intentionally for them, as for the catechumens, since, by their serious public sins, they were expelled from the Church. They would receive absolution on Holy Thursday and be reconciled with God and the community at that time.[27] This practice which originated in the Early Church would continue throughout the Middle Ages.

While this does not still take place on Holy Thursday, we should still nevertheless pray for the many lapsed and fallen away Catholics to return to the Sacrament of Confession and be restored to God's grace. During the Lenten Season, we should often pray for sinners. One great means to do so is to pray the Seven Penitential Psalms on Fridays after Matins and

Lauds, a practice that existed until the Breviary reforms of St. Pius X.

We can pray these prayers and offer our intentions along with our fasts in union with the whole Sacrifice of the Mass, for the conversion of lapsed Catholics.

Advent Fast

While not as ancient as the Holy Week fast, the Advent fast originated in the Early Church by at least the fourth century.

> The custom of keeping Advent originated in the fourth century in the churches of the East. It was only towards the end of that century that the date of Christmas was fixed for December 25th.[28]

The *Catechism of the Liturgy* describes the fast leading up to Christmas: "In a passage of St. Gregory of Tours' History of the Franks we find that St. Perpetuus, one of his predecessors in the See, had decreed in 480 AD that the faithful should fast three times a week from the feast of St. Martin (November 11th) [up] to Christmas... This period was called St. Martin's Lent and his feast was kept with the same kind of rejoicing as Carnival."[29] In historical records Advent was originally called *Quadragesimal Sancti Martini* (i.e., Forty Days Fast of St. Martin).

The *Catechism of the Liturgy* notes that this observance of fasting likely lasted until the 12th century. Remnants of this fast remained in the Roman Rite through the 19th century when Wednesday and Friday fasting in Advent continued to be mandated in most countries.

Sacramentarium Ecclesiæ Catholicæ published in 1857, states how it was practiced strictly by those under vows since Regulars refer to religious who take vows:

> About the end of the sixth century John the Faster, Patriarch of Constantinople, enforces daily abstinence from flesh during the forty days that precede the Nativity. Chrodegand, Bishop of Metz, A.D. 742 enjoins upon Regulars, daily abstinence and fast until the ninth hour from S. Martin's Day to the Nativity.[30]

The Apostles' Fast

The observance of a fast leading up to the Feast of Ss. Peter and Paul also likely originated in the Early Church. While it subsequently fell out of observance in the Roman Catholic Church, the Eastern Catholic Church still observes this fast to some extent.

The Roman Catholic Church though maintained the summer Ember Days during this time, in addition to the traditional fast on the Vigil of Saints Peter and Paul, until modern times. As a result, only a fragment of the fasting that was originally practiced persisted.

Fr. R. Janin summarizes the Traditional Byzantine Fast and Abstinence observance for the Apostles' Fast:

> This varies from 9 to 42 days depending on the feast of Easter. It begins on the first Monday after Pentecost until the feast of Saints Peter and Paul. This Lent has the same rules as Great Lent, but oil and fish are tolerated (in some places) except on Wednesdays and Fridays.[31]

Even in the Eastern Churches, there is a little divergence regarding the date when the Fast begins. The Coptic and Old Syrian traditions keep the fast on the First Monday after Pentecost (as noted above), yet in the current Byzantine tradition, the fast begins on the Second Monday after Pentecost (i.e., the day following All Saints Sunday in their calendar). This is because the Copts and Syriacs do not celebrate an octave for Pentecost. However, in any event, the origin of this fast dates to the 5th century.

The Assumption Fast

Referred to as either the Dormition Fast – since the Assumption of Our Lady is known as the Dormition by Eastern Catholics – or as the Assumption Fast, this is a two-week-long fasting period lasting from August 1st until Assumption Day. Father R. Janin writes that this fast is "a difficult Lent permitting only olives and vegetables cooked in water; oil is tolerated on Saturdays and Sundays." Like the Apostles' Fast, the Assumption Fast stretches back to the time of St. Leo the Great.

While the Assumption Fast would also fade from practice in the West, the Vigil of the Assumption on August 14th would remain a mandatory day of fasting and abstinence until 1957. Its observance as a fast day is ancient as the Catholic Encyclopedia states: "Pope Nicholas I (d. 867), in his answer to the Bulgarians, speaks of the fast on the eves of Christmas and of the Assumption...The Synod of Seligenstadt in 1022 AD mentions vigils on the eves of Christmas, Epiphany, the feast of the Apostles, the Assumption of Mary, St. Laurence, and All Saints, besides the fast of two weeks before the Nativity of St. John."[32]

One further interesting remnant of the Assumption Fast in the West is found in Sicily where the faithful would abstain from fruit for two weeks prior to the Assumption. Assumption Day is known for its blessing of herbs and fruits so the faithful, after two weeks of such abstinence, would joyfully bring their herbs and fruits to the parish for the blessing on August 15th and then, after the blessing, give each other fruit baskets.

During greater times of Latinization in the Eastern Rites in the past few centuries, the Apostles' Fast and the Dormition Fast were minimized to such an extent that they were not emphasized and not considered obligatory. About 20 years ago, the Dormition Fast was officially recognized as an important part of the Byzantine Catholic tradition but not as a fast of obligation. It was recommended that Byzantine Catholics voluntarily add Wednesday, and even Monday, as days of abstinence in addition to Friday abstinence during this period.

Lenten Fasting in the Medieval Church: 5th – 13th Century.

At the time of Pope St. Gregory the Great in the early 7th century, the fast was universally established to begin on what we know as Ash Wednesday. While the name "Ash Wednesday" was not given to the day until Pope Urban II in 1099, the day was known as the "Beginning of the Fast."

Regarding Holy Saturday's fast in particular, Canon 89 of the Council in Trullo in 692 AD provides an account of the piety and devotion of the faithful of that time: "The faithful, spending the days of the Salutatory Passion in fasting, praying and compunction of heart, ought to fast until the midnight of the Great Sabbath: since the divine Evangelists, Matthew and Luke, have shewn us how late at night it was [that the resurrection took place]." That tradition of fasting on Holy Saturday until midnight would last for centuries.

Historical records further indicate that Lent was not merely a regional practice observed only in Rome. It was part of the universality of the Church. Lenten fasting began in England, for instance, sometime during the reign of Earconberht (640 – 664), the king of Kent, who was converted by the missionary work of St. Augustine of Canterbury in England. During the Middle Ages, fasting in England, and many other then-Catholic nations, was required both by Church law and the civil law. Catholic missionaries brought fasting, which is an integral part of the Faith, to every land they visited.

Saturday Fasting in the East

In this period, controversy arose at the Council of Trullo regarding whether it was appropriate to fast on Saturdays – a practice that was observed in Rome but not elsewhere. Canon 55 of the Council states:

> Since we understand that in the city of the Romans, in the holy fast of Lent they fast on the Saturdays, contrary to the ecclesiastical observance which is traditional, it seemed good to the holy synod that also in the Church of the Romans the canon shall immovably stand fast which says: 'If any cleric shall be found to fast on a Sunday or Saturday (except on one occasion only) he is to be deposed; and if he is a layman he shall be cut off.'[33]

Importantly, the Council of Trullo (held in Constantinople) was never accepted in the West as a valid Ecumenical Council as Rome was not represented at the Council and two Canons of the Council (i.e., Canons 13 and 55) condemned certain Roman practices. But by 711 AD, Pope Constantine, in a compromise, accepted the canons in the East as valid but allowed differing practices in the Western Church to continue. A subsequent letter by Pope Hadrian I in 785 quoted Tarasios of Constantinople as approving the canons, and the letter was thereby taken as Pope Hadrian's own approval. The letter was read at the Second Council of Nicaea and in the aftermath, by the 12th century, some of the canons of the Council were incorporated in Gratian's *Decretum Gratiani*, known more commonly as the *Decretum*, which was the main source of law of the Roman Catholic Church until the *Decretals*, promulgated by Pope Gregory IX in 1234, obtained legal force.

Regarding Saturday fasting, St. Augustine had previously written:

> God did not lay down a rule concerning fasting or eating on the seventh day of the week, either at the time of His hallowing that day because in it He rested from His works, or afterwards when He gave precepts to the Hebrew nation concerning the observance of that day.[34]

Hence there were differences from East to West on when Saturday fasting was observed but St. Augustine affirms that these differences were not matters of doctrine and there was no prohibition against Saturday fasting in divine law and no universal obligation in the Church to fast year-round on Saturdays either. St. Augustine further writes on this disagreement while noting the binding force of custom:

> As to the question on which you wish my opinion, whether it is lawful to fast on the seventh day of the week, I answer, that if it were wholly unlawful, neither Moses nor Elijah, nor our Lord himself, would have fasted for forty successive days. But by the same argument it is proved that even on the Lord's Day fasting is not unlawful. And yet, if any one was to think that the Lord's Day should be appointed a day of fasting, in the same way as the seventh day is observed by some, such a

man would be regarded, and not unjustly, as bringing a great cause of offence into the Church. For in those things concerning which the divine Scriptures have laid down no definitive rule, the custom of the people of God, or the practices instituted by their fathers, are to be held as the law of the Church. If we choose to fall into a debate about these things, and to denounce one party merely because their custom differs from that of others, the consequence must be an endless contention, in which the utmost care is necessary lest the storm of conflict overcast with clouds the calmness of brotherly love, while the strength is spent in mere controversy which cannot adduce on either side any decisive testimonies of truth.[35]

In the East, the issue long preceded the Council of Trullo and was based on the sabbath having been a day for rest and prayer similar, though distinct, from Sunday. This tradition is seen in the Apostolic Constitutions:

But assemble yourselves together every day, morning and evening, singing psalms and praying in the Lord's house: in the morning saying the sixty second Psalm, and in the evening the hundred and fortieth, but principally on the Sabbath-day. And of the day of our Lord's resurrection, which is the Lord's Day, meet more diligently, sending praise to God that made the universe by Jesus, and sent him to us, and condescended to let him suffer, and raised Him from the dead. Otherwise, what apology will he make to God who does not assemble on that day to hear the saving word concerning resurrection?[36]

Yet the same Council of Trullo in Canon 56 shows the universality of the form of abstinence in both East and West at that time:

> We have likewise learned that in the regions of Armenia and in other places certain people eat eggs and cheese on the Sabbaths and Lord's days of the holy Lent. It seems good therefore that the whole Church of God which is in all the world should follow one rule and keep the fast perfectly, and as they abstain from everything which is killed, so also should they from eggs and cheese, which are the fruit and produce of those animals from which we abstain. But if any shall not observe this law, if they be clerics, let them be deposed; but if laymen, let them be cut off.[37]

The controversy would continue when in 867, the patriarch of Constantinople, Photius, wrote an encyclical to the other patriarchs of the Eastern churches, accusing the Roman Catholic Church of several errors alleging among them Saturday fasting and "giving permission to the people to eat flesh food and animal products (cheese, milk, eggs) during the first week of Easter."[38]

Photius audaciously issued an attempted excommunication of the Pope, for which he was condemned and deposed as Francis Dvornik notes:

> By daring to pass judgment on a Pope, Photius committed a deed till then unheard of in history, one that endangered the unity of Christendom, for which there could be neither excuse nor justification. Rightly or wrongly, his action set a precedent invoked or imitated

by all those who later were to break the unity of the Church.[39]

The Binding Force of Custom

The tension regarding fasting and abstinence would continue to intensify and would unfortunately be one of several factors that would lead to the Great Schism of 1054 between the Orthodox and the Catholic Church. However, the tensions of this time highlight the misunderstanding of the binding force of custom.

St. Augustine further addressed this point directly when he writes: "The customs of God's people and the institutions of our ancestors are to be considered as laws. And those who throw contempt on the customs of the Church ought to be punished as those who disobey the law of God."[40] St. Thomas likewise asserts: "Custom has the force of law, abrogates law, and interprets law."[41] As previously noted, fasting on Wednesday and Friday was previously obligatory by custom before it became obligatory by decree under St. Perpetuus.

Fasting in Septuagesima (i.e., Pre-Lent)

In both the East and the West, the weeks immediately before Lent were kept as a period of preparation for the austere fasting that started with Great Lent. This period in the West, up until Vatican II in the 1960s, was called Septuagesima.

The force of custom concerning fasting is also seen in the churches in Gaul in modern-day France who adopted the Roman practice of fasting on Saturday. Dom Guéranger mentions this while also noting how changes were likewise occurring in terms of where and how the fast of Septuagesima began:

The first Council of Orleans, held in the early part of the 6th century, enjoins the Faithful [of Gaul] to observe, before Easter, Quadragesima, (as the Latins call Lent,) and not Quinquagesima, in order, says the Council, that unity of custom may be maintained. Towards the close of the same century, the fourth Council held in the same City repeals the same prohibition, and explains the intentions of making such an enactment, by ordering that the Saturdays during Lent should be observed as days of fasting. Previously to this, that is, in the years 511 and 541, the first and second Councils of Orange had combated the same abuse, by also forbidding the imposing on the Faithful the obligation of commencing the Fast at Quinquagesima. The introduction of the Roman Liturgy into France, which was brought about by the zeal of Pepin and Charlemagne, finally established, in that country, the custom of keeping the Saturday as a day of penance; and, as we have just seen, the beginning of Lent on Quinquagesima was not observed excepting by the Clergy. In the 13th century, the only Church in the Patriarchate of the West, which began Lent earlier than the Church of Rome, was that of Poland. Its Lent opened on the Monday of Septuagesima, which was owing to the rites of the Greek Church being much used in Poland. The custom was abolished, even in that country, by Pope Innocent the fourth, in the year 1248.[42]

Septuagesima is both the name of the third Sunday before Lent as well as the season itself that runs from this day up until Ash Wednesday. The other Sundays in the Season of Septuagesima are Sexagesima Sunday and Quinquagesima Sunday.

Septuagesima is an appropriate time for us to begin preparing our bodies for the upcoming Lenten fast by incorporating some fasting into our routine. In some places a custom of observing a fast of devotion, in anticipation of and in preparation for the Great Lenten fast, was observed as Father Weiser mentions in his *Handbook of Christian Feasts and Customs*:

> This preparatory time of pre-Lent in the Latin Church was suggested by the practice of the Byzantine Church, which started its great fast earlier, because their 'forty days' did not include Saturdays. Saint Maximum (465 AD), Bishop of Turin, mentioned the practice in one of his sermons. It is a pious custom, he said, to keep a fast of devotion (not of obligation) before the start of Lent.[43]

Collations Are Introduced on Fasting Days

The rules on fasting remained largely the same for hundreds of years. Food was to be taken once a day after sunset. After the meal, the fast resumed and was terminated only after the sun had once again set on the horizon. But relaxations were soon to begin.

By the eighth century, the time for the daily meal was moved to the time that the monks would pray the Office of None in the Divine Office. This office takes place around 3 o'clock in the afternoon. Because of moving the meal up in the day, the practice of a collation was introduced. The well-researched Father Francis Xavier Weiser summarizes this major change with fasting:

> It was not until the ninth century, however, that less rigid laws of fasting were introduced. It came about in 817 when the monks of the Benedictine order, who did much labor in the fields and on the farms, were allowed to take a little drink with a morsel of bread in the evening... Eventually the Church extended the new laws to the laity as well, and by the end of the medieval times they had become universal practice; everybody ate a little evening meal in addition to the main meal at noon.[44]

According to Butler originally the collation was only water mixed with a little wine.[45] When the custom first arose in monasteries the amount of water allotted was about a pint. The monks called it a draught. This was not practiced before the 9th century and even after the 9th century it was not until the 14th century that water and other liquids were allowed to all classes of people outside the meal on fast days. Early on, only monks had this privilege. Eventually it was extended to clerics and then finally to laity. Food being allowed in the collation did not arise until the 15th century when only a couple of ounces was allowed. But the origin of the collation dates back to 817 AD.

How was Lenten Abstinence Observed?

In 604, in a letter to St. Augustine of Canterbury, Pope St. Gregory the Great announced the form that abstinence would take on fast days. This form would last for almost a thousand years: "We abstain from flesh meat and from all things that come from flesh, as milk, cheese, and eggs."[46] When fasting was observed, abstinence was likewise always observed. Sometime between the time of St. Gregory the Great and St. Thomas Aquinas abstinence on non-Lenten days began to permit the consumption of animal products like eggs and dairy. Only flesh meat was prohibited. This change, however, did not impact Lenten days of abstinence, which retained the strictness of former times.

Through the writings of St. Thomas Aquinas, we can learn how Lent was practiced in his own time and attempt to willingly observe such practices in our own lives. The Lenten fast as mentioned by St. Thomas Aquinas consisted of the following:

- Monday through Saturday were days of fasting. The meal was taken at 3 PM and a collation was allowed at night.
- All meat or animal products were prohibited throughout Lent.
- Abstinence from these foods remained even on Sundays of Lent, though fasting was not practiced on Sundays.[47]
- If possible, one could strive to consume no food on either Ash Wednesday or Good Friday, which harkened back to the Passion Fast practiced in the Early Church.

- Holy Week was a more intense fast that consisted only of bread, salt, water, and herbs.

The Lenten fast included fasting from all *lacticinia* (Latin for milk products) which included butter, cheese, eggs, and all similar animal products. From this tradition, Easter Eggs were introduced, and therefore the Tuesday before Ash Wednesday is when pancakes are traditionally eaten to use leftover *lacticinia*. And similarly, Fat Tuesday is known as Carnival, coming from the Latin words *carne levare* – literally the "farewell to meat."

Regarding this point, there are important exceptions to note as the Church has always exercised common sense. Father Weiser notes that "Abstinence from *lacticinia* which included milk, butter, cheese, and eggs, was never strictly enforced in…Scandinavia because of the lack of oil and other substitute foods in those countries. The Church, using common sense, granted many dispensations in this matter in all countries of Europe. People who did eat the milk foods would often, when they could afford it, give alms for the building of churches or other pious endeavors."[48]

The words of Pope Innocent III who reigned during this era from January 1198 to July 1216 before the Fourth Lateran Council apply as much to us as to those who lived during the 13th century: "To your praying add fasting and almsgiving. It is on these wings that our prayers fly the more swiftly and effortlessly to the holy ears of God, that He may mercifully hear us in the time of need."[49]

Abstinence from Sexual Activity in Lent

Through the Middle Ages, the faithful also abstained from sexual relations during the whole of Lent,[50] as evidenced by birth records showing a drastic decrease in births 9 months after Lent. In Spain, the custom of abstaining from sexual relations was widely practiced well into the mid-1900s and did not widely end until the completion of Franco's rule.[51] While not part of Roman Catholic fasting rules, the Eastern Orthodox Church continues to require abstinence from sexual relations during Lent. Similarly, the Ukrainian Catholic Church counsels:

> Married couples are expected to abstain from the marital embrace throughout the Church's four fasting seasons as well as on the weekly Wednesday and Friday fasts and the Communion fast. This aspect of the fasting rule is probably even more widely ignored, and more difficult for many, than those relating to food. In recognition of this, some sources advocate a more modest, minimal rule: couples should abstain from the marital embrace before receiving Holy Communion and throughout Holy Week.[52]

Black Fasting

A commonly misunderstood aspect of fasting is the "black fast." What is the true definition of a black fast? And what is it not? The Catholic Encyclopedia from 1907 answers as follows:

> This form of fasting, the most rigorous in the history of church legislation, was marked by austerity regarding the quantity and quality of food permitted on fasting days as well as the time wherein such food might be legitimately taken.[53]

This is based in practice on the fasting done by the Early Church and the Apostles. In practice, there are three criteria that make a fast a "black fast" as the Encyclopedia identifies:

In the first place more than one meal was strictly prohibited. At this meal flesh meat, eggs, butter, cheese, and milk were interdicted (Gregory I, Decretals IV, cap. vi; Trullan Synod, Canon 56). Besides these restrictions, abstinence from wine, especially during Lent, was enjoined (Thomassin, Traité des jeûnes de l'Église, II, vii). Furthermore, during Holy Week the fare consisted of bread, salt, herbs, and water (Laymann, Theologia Moralis, Tr. VIII; De observatione jejuniorum, i). Finally, this meal was not allowed until sunset. St. Ambrose (De Elia et jejunio, sermo vii, in Psalm CXVIII), St. Chrysostom (Homil. iv in Genesim), St. Basil (Oratio i, De jejunio) furnish unequivocal testimony concerning the three characteristics of the black fast.[54]

Hence a black fast is one that meets these criteria:

1. Only one meal a day
2. Complete abstinence from all meat and animal products
3. The one meal may only be consumed after sunset.

Consequently, it is not a total abstinence from all food and drink whatsoever that makes a fast a "black fast". And it also does not mean that one eats only bread. Vegetables are certainly allowed at the meal.

A Feast in Proportion to the Fast

As the holiest of all Christian holy days, it is fitting that Easter is rife with customs after the end of the Lenten fast, and many of these customs originate back at least as far as the Middle Ages.

While cultures may vary in how they observe Easter, a unifying theme throughout is found in food. After having completed forty strict days of fasting and forty-six days of abstinence, Easter ushers in a period of fifty days where the faithful celebrate through various meats, eggs, dairy products, and other foods which were forbidden in Lent. On Holy Saturday, the custom originated for the faithful to bring their Easter foods to church where the priest would bless them. The Roman Ritual still provides a beautiful blessing of Easter food in the form of blessings of lamb, eggs, bread, and new produce.

Which foods were found in Easter baskets varied from culture to culture. In Slavic regions, ham was often the main dish because of its richness and serving it was a symbol of joy and abundance at Easter. But lamb and veal were found too. But in any case, the meats were often cooked together so as not to burden the cooks with too much preparation on such a great holy day. In Hungary, Easter is referred to as the "Feast of Meat" (Husvet), because the eating of meat resumes after the long fast of Lent.

Because of having traditionally abstained from all butter, eggs, and cheese, these foods were often found in baskets as well. We see this first and foremost in the continued tradition of Easter eggs. A person truly appreciates Easter eggs only after having abstained from eggs for 46 days. After such a time, having an egg is truly a treat! Russian eggs are traditionally dyed red due to a story dating back to St. Mary Magdalene, but other cultures have chosen to paint even elaborate symbols on the eggs. The story is told that St. Mary Magdalene preached the Gospel to a doubter who asked for a miracle – prompting a white egg to turn red. The red egg also symbolizes the Passion, which, after it is broken shows the egg white, which symbolizes the Resurrection.

As another item formerly forbidden in Lent, cheese is a great treat to those who have abstained from it for the 46 days of abstinence. The Russians would customarily make a custard type of cheese that was shaped into a ball. Known for its bland but sweet taste, it was meant to indicate that it is fitting that Christians should still engage in moderation and never gluttony even in Eastertide. And on this point, Fr. Goffine expresses similar rationale for why the Church enriches such customs with blessings from the Roman Ritual:

> Why does the Church on this day bless eggs, bread, and meat? To remind the faithful that although the time of fasting is now ended, they should not indulge in gluttony, but thank God, and use their food simply for the necessary preservation of physical strength.[55]

Russian Easter baskets will often feature salt as a reminder of our Lord's own words to his disciples that it is their duty to be the "salt of the earth" (cf. Matthew 5:13). The baskets may also hold horseradish, which symbolizes the passion of Christ yet, when mixed with sugar, helps us see how the Resurrection has sweetened the Passion of Christ. Indeed, the details indicate to us how cultures valued and celebrated the Resurrection with intricate attention to detail. Even the butter in some baskets would be shaped into the figure of a small lamb or at least decorated in stick form with the image of a cross on the top.

Fast Free Periods in the East

It should also be noted that in Eastern Orthodoxy there is no fasting even on Wednesday and Friday in the 7 weeks between Easter and Pentecost. For the Ukrainian Catholic Church, like the Byzantine Catholic Church, there are four fast-free periods:

1. Christmas (Dec. 25) to the Eve of Theophany (Jan 5)

2. The week following the Sunday of the Publican and Pharisee
3. Bright Week which is known as "Easter Week" in the West
4. Trinity Week, the week after Pentecost, ends with All Saints Sunday.

In the Eastern Catholic Rites, as in Eastern Orthodoxy, fasting and abstinence are synonymous so no abstinence is practiced these weeks as well.

Rogation Days

Besides the Lenten fast, the traditions of Rogation Days, Ember Days, and the Advent fast developed in the Church throughout the Middle Ages.

The Rogation Days occur on four days each year: the Major Rogation (i.e., Greater Litanies) on April 25th and the Minor Rogation Days (i.e., Lesser Litanies) on the Monday, Tuesday, and Wednesday before Ascension Thursday. These days have virtually disappeared now as only Traditional Catholic priests keep them. However, for those who do keep these days, they are days to pray in a special way. The Litany of the Saints is especially prayed on these days and crops and field are blessed.

Concerning the Major Rogation, Dom Guéranger, writing in the late 1800s, mentions the ancient custom of abstinence but not fasting for the Major Rogation:

> Abstinence from flesh meat has always been observed on this day at Rome; and when the Roman Liturgy was established in France by Pepin and Charlemagne, the Great Litany of April 25 was, of course, celebrated, and the abstinence kept by the faithful of that country.

A Council of Aix-la-Chapelle, in 836, enjoined the additional obligation of resting from servile work on this day: the same enactment is found in the Capitularia of Charles the Bald. As regards fasting, properly so-called, being contrary to the spirit of Paschal Time, it would seem never to have been observed on this day, at least not generally. Amalarius, who lived in the ninth century, asserts that it was not then practiced even in Rome.[56]

Dom Guéranger likewise continues with an account of how fasting and abstinence were kept on the Minor Rogation Days:

Their observance is now similar in format to the Greater Litanies of April 25th, but these three days have a different origin, having been instituted in Gaul in the fifth century as days of fasting, abstinence, and abstention from servile work in which all took part in an extensive penitential procession, often barefoot. The whole western Church soon adopted the Rogation days. They were introduced into England at an early period, as likewise into Spain and Germany. Rome herself sanctioned them by herself observing them; this she did in the eighth century, during the pontificate of St. Leo III. With regard to the fast which the Churches of Gaul observed during the Rogation days, Rome did not adopt that part of the institution. Fasting seemed to her to throw a gloom over the joyous forty days, which our risen Jesus grants to His disciples; she therefore enjoined only abstinence from flesh-meat during the Rogation days.[57]

The Minor Rogation Days date back to 470 AD when Bishop Mamertus of Vienne in Gaul instituted an annual observance of penance on the three days immediately before the Feast of the Ascension. He prescribed litanies in the form of processions for all three days. Thereafter they spread to the Frankish part of France in 511, to Spain in the 6th century, and to the German part of the Frankish empire in 813. In 816, Pope Leo III incorporated the lesser litanies into the Roman Liturgy, and during the subsequent centuries the annual custom of holding these litanies took root.

While the Lesser Litanies (i.e., Minor Rogation Days) are kept on the three days leading up to Ascension Day, Father Francis Weiser notes an important exception for the 19th Century: "Pope Pius XII granted to some Catholic missions in the Pacific Islands the permission to celebrate both the major and minor litanies in October or November."[58]

Hence from ancient times the Church has kept these days as days of supplication. And even if fasting, the hallmark of Lent, would seem to be ill-suited for Pascaltide, abstinence is still permitted and was even obligatory in some places on the Rogation Days. In fact, English Catholics kept all four Rogation Days as days of mandatory abstinence as late as 1830 until they were dispensed by Pope Pius VIII.[59]

Ember Days

The Angelus Press 1962 Roman Catholic Daily Missal provides a succinct summary of Ember Days for the faithful:

> At the beginning of the four seasons of the Ecclesiastical Year, the Ember Days have been instituted by the Church to thank God for blessings obtained during the past year and to implore further graces for the new season. Their importance in the Church was formerly

very great. They are fixed on the Wednesday, Friday, and Saturday: after the First Sunday of Lent for spring, after Pentecost Sunday for summer, after the Feast of the Exaltation of the Cross (14th September) for autumn, and after the Third Sunday of Advent for winter. They are intended, too, to consecrate to God the various seasons in nature, and to prepare by penance those who are about to be ordained. Ordinations generally take place on the Ember Days. The faithful ought to pray on these days for good priests. The Ember Days were until c. 1960 fastdays of obligation.[60]

Hence Ember days were categorized by three elements: prayers for both thanksgiving and petition, penance in the form of fasting and abstinence, and ordinations. Like Rogation Days, Ember Days developed early in these times, taking the form that would continue for centuries. *The Catholic Encyclopedia* explains:

At first the Church in Rome had fasts in June, September, and December; the exact days were not fixed but were announced by the priests. The Liber Pontificalis ascribes to Pope Callistus (217 – 222) a law ordering the fast, but probably it is older. Leo the Great (440 – 461) considers it an Apostolic institution.[61]

By the time of Pope Gregory I, who died in 601 AD, they were observed for all four seasons though the date of each of them could vary. In the Roman Synod of 1078 under Pope Gregory VII, they were uniformly established for the Wednesday, Friday, and Saturday after December 13th (St. Lucia), after Ash Wednesday, after Pentecost Sunday, and after September 14th (Exaltation of the Cross). While they were initially observed only in Rome, their observance quickly spread as the Catholic Encyclopedia further adds:

> Before Gelasius the ember days were known only in Rome, but after his time their observance spread. They were brought into England by St. Augustine; into Gaul and Germany by the Carlovingians. Spain adopted them with the Roman Liturgy in the eleventh century. They were introduced by St. Charles Borromeo into Milan. The Eastern Church does not know them. The present Roman Missal, in the formulary for the Ember days, retains in part the old practice of lessons from Scripture in addition to the ordinary two: for the Wednesdays three, for the Saturdays six, and seven for the Saturday in December. Some of these lessons contain promises of a bountiful harvest for those that serve God.[62]

Dom Prosper Guéranger adds that the institution of the Ember Days is further based on the fast ordered by God for the changing of the seasons in the Old Testament. Thus, the Church hallowed that fast and adopted it for the worship of the True God thus fulfilling the Lord's words that He came not to abolish but to complete (cf. Matthew 5:17) what was instituted in the Old Testament:

> We may consider it as one of those practices which the Church took from the Synagogue; for the prophet Zacharias speaks of the fasts of the fourth, fifth, seventh, and tenth months. Its introduction into the Christian Church would seem to have been made in the apostolic times; such, at least, is the opinion of St. Leo, of St. Isidore of Seville, of Rabanus Maurus, and of several other ancient Christian writers. It is

remarkable, on the other hand, that the Orientals do not observe this fast.[63]

Changes in the time of the meal also occurred over the centuries shifting by not only the time of the meal earlier in the day but also by distinguishing the time of fasting on weekly devotional fasts as opposed to other days of fasting like Lenten days and Ember Days. In a change to the time of fasting in the ancient Roman Church, the fast was broken at sunset for Ember Days but the weekly devotional fasts changed to 3 PM.

> A second part of this duty and precept is the fast itself, which is a retrenching of ordinary meals, and a forbearance of all food for a time: it essentially requires that a person confine himself to one temperate meal in the day. The hour of taking it was anciently after sunset. Whence the Fathers reproached the slothful and lukewarm Christians, that they seemed to think the days were too long, and the sunset too late in Lent. This discipline was observed not only in Lent, but also on Ember days, vigils, and other fasting days, except the weekly fasts of Wednesdays and Fridays, on which the meal was taken at noon, or three o'clock in the afternoon. On which account they were distinguished by the name of the fasts of the stations, and demi-feasts...[by] the thirteenth century, the hour of noon, or three o'clock, is determined by all the pastors of the church and doctors of the schools for the time on which it was lawful for those who fast to take their meal.[64]

Spirituality of the Ember Days

The purpose of Ember Days is, in the words of the Catholic Encyclopedia, to "thank God for the gifts of nature, to teach men to make use of them in moderation, and to assist the needy." As a result, their focus differs from the precise focus of the Rogation Days to which they are often compared.

In addition to the general purpose of thanking God and invoking His blessings, the author of *Barefoot Abbey* provides specific intentions for each of these seasons so that we can render thanks to Almighty God for the fruits of the earth which specifically become instruments of His grace through the Sacraments:

> Winter or Advent Ember Days are after the Feast of St. Lucy (December 13th): Give thanks for the olives that make holy oils for Unction. Spring or Lenten Ember Days are after Ash Wednesday: Give thanks for the flowers and bees that make blessed candles as in for Baptism and upon the alter. Summer or Whit Ember Days are after the Solemnity of Pentecost: Give thanks for the wheat used to make the Eucharist hosts. Autumn or Michaelmas Ember Days are after the Feast of Exaltation of the Holy Cross (September 14): Give thanks for the grapes that make wine for the Precious Blood of Christ.[65]

By writing these down and recalling them for the Ember Days of each season, we can be more intentional in what we are thanking God for in any given season. In this respect, the Ember Days further distinguish themselves from the Rogation Days.

The Cultural Impact of the Ember Days to Japan

Ember Days are not a relic of the Ancient or Medieval Church only – they would remain obligatory for the faithful until the changes immediately after Vatican II in the mid-1960s. In fact, their occurrence is the reason we have "tempura" dishes in some Asian dishes. For instance, shrimp tempura is based on Ember Days, which are known as quatuor tempora in Latin).

Portuguese (and Spanish) missionaries to the Far East would invite the converted Japanese to fast during the quatuor tempora by eating a dish that consisted of battered and deep-fried seafood and vegetables called "Peixinhos da Horta" in Portuguese which literally translated to "little fishes from the garden." It was a dish consisting of bell peppers, squash, and green beans that is fried into a flour-based batter. The term steadily gained popularity in southern Japan and became widely used to refer to any sort of food prepared using hot oil, battered or not. This term would persist even after Catholicism was outlawed by the Japanese and the Church's missionaries were executed or exiled in the late 1500s. It was not until the 1870s that Christianity legally returned to Japan. But the faithful of Japan continued to keep the Faith alive in their families, including through the keeping of fast and abstinence days.

The Advent Fast (St. Martin's Lent)

As previously mentioned, the Advent Fast began in the Early Church and developed over the centuries. The fast which appeared in 480 began to adopt the same rigor of Lent by the end of the 6th century when the fast was extended to the whole Church and priests were instructed to offer Mass during St. Martin's Lent, as it was then called, according to the Lenten rite.

By the 700s, the observance was shortened in the Roman Rite to four weeks, though other rites maintained the longer observance. By the 1100s, the fast had begun to be replaced by simple abstinence. *Sacramentarium Ecclesiæ Catholicæ* states:

> Peter the Venerable, the ninth Abbot of Cluny, A.D. 1123, says, 'Since a more than ordinary abstinence is kept by nearly the whole Church on these days, in order to prepare for the Nativity of the Lord, let us consecrate these hallowed days with moderate fasts, which many others consecrate with greater fasts.'[66]

The writer continues:

> Although the period is forty days, there never were anywhere actually forty fast days, because fasting was prohibited on Sabbaths, except at Rome, and everywhere on Lord's Days. There could therefore be only twenty-eight, twenty-nine or third fast days within the period. And as the Roman Church allowed fasting on Sabbaths, the period was shortened by five or six days, according to the number of Sabbaths...

> Some severe monastic orders, e.g., the friars minors, did actually observe forty fast days, and so began this Lent after the Octave of All Saints, which allows forty fast days exclusive of Sabbaths and Lord's Days...[67]

In 1281, the Council of Salisbury held that only monks were expected to keep the fast; however, in a revival of the older practice, Pope Urban V in 1362 required abstinence for all members of the papal court during Advent.[68] However, the custom of fasting in Advent shortly thereafter continued its decline.

We should do our part at rediscovering Advent by observing the Nativity Fast, as it is still practiced to some extent in the Byzantine Catholic Church, starting on the day after the Feast of St. Martin (i.e., Martinmas) on November 11th. Some Byzantine traditions will refer to the fast as the Quadragesima of Saint Philip since it begins immediately after their feastday in honor of the Apostle St. Philip.

Even closer to our modern times, remnants of St. Martin's Lent remained in the Roman Rite through the 19th century when Wednesday and Friday fasting in Advent continued to be mandated in some countries. In the United States, fasting was kept on the Wednesdays and Fridays of Advent, as was the Universal practice of the Church, until 1840 when the fast on Wednesdays in Advent was abrogated for Americans. The fast on Fridays in Advent was abrogated in 1917 in America and abroad with the promulgation of the 1917 Code of Canon Law.

The Code similarly removed the Wednesdays of Advent for any localities that continued to mandate them as well as the Saturdays of Advent which were kept elsewhere, such as in Italy, as evident by a 1906 decree which mandated the fast. Father Villien comments, "This discipline, which at the present day is observed by Italy alone among the nations of the West, is the last vestige of a very ancient fast, the fast of Advent."[69]

But even the attempts to maintain elements of the Advent fast from the 17th through the 20th centuries were shadows of St. Martin's Lent. In fact, the Church still encouraged people to keep the venerable discipline of St. Martin's Lent, even if it was not obligatory under pain of sin. This fact is expressed with conviction in the Catechism of Perseverance:

> The Church neglects no means of revisiting in
> her children the fervor of their ancestors. Is it
> not just? Is the little Babe whom we expect less

beautiful, less holy, less worthy of our love now than formerly? Has He ceased to be the Friend of pure hearts? Is His coming into our souls less needed? Alas! perhaps we have raised there all the idols that, eighteen centuries ago, He came to overturn. Let us therefore be more wise. Let us enter into the views of the Church: let us consider how this tender mother redoubles her solicitude to form in us those dispositions of penance and charity which are necessary for a proper reception of the Babe of Bethlehem.[70]

On this point, Father Villien concurs:

But it is only with regret that the Church permits her institutions to disappear. She wishes to retain at least a vestige of them as a witness to a former stage of development. This is what she has done for Italy by the decree of September 7, 1906.[71]

Fasting in Honor of the Holy Innocents

Even after the commencement of Christmas, the Church continued to mandate abstinence on the Friday in the Octave of Christmas. This was also seen in the Middle Ages in the form of a fast from foods cooked in fats on the Feast of the Holy Innocents on December 28th, at a time even when the Feast of the Holy Innocents was a Holy Day of Obligation. Prior to the changes in the Mass under Pope Pius XII in the mid-1950s the priest would wear purple vestments, and not red ones, on the Feast of the Holy Innocents. In Mass both the Gloria in Excelsis and the Alleluias were omitted. However, as Helen McLoughlin notes in her book on Catholic customs: "And yet there is joy in her services. Children sing with the choirs in the great cathedrals; and in ancient times other functions were given to them — hence the name 'Childermas' or Children's Mass."[72]

At some point in the past, at least in one place, there was a fast and abstinence from flesh meat and foods cooked in fats on Holy Innocents Day. As Cardinal Schuster notes in *The Sacramentary*:

> The *Ordines Romani* prescribe that the Pope and his assistants should be arrayed in purple vestments, that the deacons and subdeacons should put on the processional paenula, and that the Pontiff should wear a miter of plain white linen. The Te Deum was not sung at the night office, nor were the Gloria and the Alleluia at the Mass, unless it were a Sunday, while the faithful were bidden to abstain from flesh meat and from foods cooked in fats. In the fifteenth century, however, the pontifical court used to celebrate this feast in the papal chapel, a sermon being preached for the occasion; but little by little this tradition died out, as the *Ordines Romani* XIV and XV sadly lament.[73]

Both Cardinal Schuster and Fr. Lasance mention the fast, which would seem appropriate in honor of the children who were martyred on this day. This is a worthwhile optional practice we may want to do as well, and we can offer up this penance for the souls of the unborn, even though this fast faded away long before the Liturgy was changed in the mid-20th century.

St. Michael's Lent

St. Bonaventure records in his biography (written between 1260-1266) how St. Francis of Assisi, "was brought after many and varied toils unto a high mountain apart, that is called

Mount Alverna. When, according unto his wont, he began to keep a Lent there, fasting, in honor of St. Michael Archangel, he was filled unto overflowing, and as never before, with the sweetness of heavenly contemplation."[74]

The *Little Flowers of St. Francis*, a collection of stories about St. Francis that was compiled during the 13th century, records these words of St. Francis to his brothers: "My sons, we are drawing nigh to our forty days' fast of St. Michael the Archangel; and I firmly believe that it is the will of God that we keep this fast in the mountain of Alvernia, the which by Divine dispensation hath been made ready for us, to the end that we may, through penance, merit from Christ the consolation of consecrating that blessed mountain to the honor and glory of God and of His glorious mother, the Virgin Mary, and of the holy angels."[75]

This fasting period was one of devotion and was not kept by reason of obligation in the Universal Church or any diocese, from what it seems. Yet, nevertheless, it underscores the devotion and fervor that existed and was about to steadily erode further after the Renaissance.

The Fall of Catholic Fasting: Post-Renaissance

Fasting in the Renaissance: 13th – mid 18th Century

As the Middle Ages ended and the Renaissance emerged, the piety and devotion of many souls likewise became tempered. The Church underwent significant trials in these centuries including the Protestant Revolt and the loss of hundreds of thousands of souls, yet She also found new children in lands previously undiscovered. Yet even amid these changes, the Church did continue to encourage fasting – even on days beyond those mandated for the entire Church. For instance, as mentioned in *the Raccolta* for Corpus Christi:

> Pope Urban IV... being desirous that all the faithful should give God due thanks for this inestimable benefit and be excited to meet their Lord's love in this most holy Sacrament with grateful hearts, granted in the said Constitution several Indulgences to the faithful, which were again augmented by Pope Martin V in his Constitution *Ineffabile* of May 26, 1429. Afterwards Pope Eugenius IV, in his Constitution *Excellentissimum* of May 20, 1433, confirmed the Indulgences of Martin V, and added others, as follows: An indulgence of 200 days, on the vigil of the Feast of Corpus Christi to all who, being truly contrite and having confessed, shall fast, or do some other good work enjoined them by their confessor...[76]

Concerning indulgences, partial indulgences were measured in days or years before the changes imposed after Vatican II. This time referred to an equivalent number of days or years of penance that would be remitted. For example, an indulgence of 200 days for the above mentioned fast would cancel out the same amount of temporal punishment that would have been remitted had a person in the state of grace done 200 days of prescribed penance (e.g., the canonical penance in the early Church). Indulgences are thus a truly effective means to remit the temporal punishment due to sin. For a truly minimal amount of effort, months or years of penance can be mitigated.

Norbertine Fasting Mitigations

Religious orders were not immune from the tendency to mitigate the ancient discipline of fasting and abstinence. This is seen for instance with the mitigations introduced for the Premonstratensian Rite founded by St. Norbert (1080 – 1134 AD). The following history of the mitigations of this time, which were happening in other religious orders is recounted by Joseph Gribbin:

> As a result of divergent and seemingly 'illicit' practices concerning the use of fish and dairy products on Mondays and Wednesdays, a provincial chapter (1495) decreed that flesh meat was to be eaten twice on those days...It was forbidden in Advent, Lent (after Sexagesima Sunday) and at other times which were prescribed by the Church. These stipulations reflect the mitigations in meat eating which were prevalent in monasticism in general; though legislation on this matter varied among the religious orders. The regulations of the 1495 English provincial chapter went beyond the statutes, which generally forbade eating flesh-meat, but more or less paralleled the mandated and proposed mitigations of their continental brethren. A bull of Pope Pius II, which was promulgated in 1464, confirmed the decisions of the Premonstratensian general chapter to abstain from meat on Wednesdays and Saturdays each week, on the vigils of the four principal feasts of the Church, during the season of Advent, and from Septuagesima to Easter. In 1499 the general chapter at Saint Quentin sought papal permission to eat meat 'omni tempore,' except on Wednesdays and Saturdays, during Advent,

and the period from Septuagesima until Easter. Presumably these documents tacitly assumed Friday abstinence.[77]

Contrast this with the practice of St. Norbert as recounted in the Roman Breviary: "He ate only once a day, in the evening, and then his meal was of Lenten fare. His life was of singular austerity, and he used, even in the depth of winter, to go out with bare feet and ragged garments. Hence came that mighty power of his words and deeds, whereby he was enabled to turn countless heretics to the faith, sinners to repentance, and enemies to peace and concord."

The Spanish Crusade Bulls

Known as the "Bula de Cruzada" (Spanish for Crusade Bulls), they were a series of papal bulls issued as far back as 1089 but which continued throughout the centuries with bulls issued in 1118, 1197, 1478, 1479, 1481, 1482, 1485, 1494, 1503 and 1505.

In 1089 Pope Urban II granted a dispensation to Spain from abstinence on Fridays, in virtue of the Spanish efforts in the Crusades to expel the Muslims from the southern half of Spain and thus end the persecution of Mozarabic Christians in that region. This would be the first Crusade Bull. On this and the ensuing bulls, the author of *Dei Praesidio Suffulus* writes:

> On 10 December 1118, Gelasius II acceded to the request of King Alphonsus I of Aragón, granting spiritual favors to those who would participate in the reconquest of Zaragoza, in the form of a plenary indulgence. On 4 April 1122, Callistus II sent a bull to all bishops and Christian princes to aid the kings of Spain in their crusade against the Muslims of Iberia. This was made possible through the efforts of

Saint Ollegar, archbishop of Tarragona, whose feast day was kept in the Philippine Church on 6 March, who made a pilgrimage to the Holy Land in the same year the bull was sent.

Count Raymond Berengar IV of Barcelona completed the reconquest of Tortosa in 1148 and thereupon asked Eugene III to consider it a Crusade, which request the pope granted on 22 June 1148, decorating it with indulgences. The next bull came out before the miraculous victory obtained by King Alphonsus VIII of Navarra in the Battle of Las Navas de Tolosa on 16 July 1212, the same victory which is celebrated in the feast of the Triumph of the Holy Cross, proper to Spain and her former colonies, kept in the liturgical calendar of the Philippines on 16 July (necessitating the transfer of the feast of Our Lady of Mount Carmel to 21 July). The reconquest was preceded by solemn rogations in Rome, led by Innocent III on 23 May 1212, days before which, he sent a letter to the king, granting him the spiritual favors he asked of the pope through his ambassador in Rome.[78]

After the Battle of Lepanto in 1571, Pope St. Pius V expanded that privilege to all Spanish colonies. That dispensation remained in place in some places as late as 1951 when the Archdiocese of Santa Fe in New Mexico, the last territory to invoke it, rescinded the privilege.

The original purpose of the bull was to reward those who wished to contribute to the Crusade efforts, yet the bull continued to be in effect for centuries as Father Slater summarizes:

The bulla cruciatæ, or Bull of the Crusade, was a papal Bull which originally granted indulgences in favor of those who took part in the wars against the Moors in Spain. Those who could not fight against the infidel could help in the good work by contributing money, and those who did this were admitted to a share in the privileges granted by the Bull. The Bull continued to be granted after the crusades ceased, and the proceeds derived therefrom were devoted to the building of churches and other pious objects.[79]

One provision of these bulls served to dispense the faithful from fasting and abstinence during Lent. The first bull of meat at the state level was delivered by Pope Julius II to the Catholic Monarchs in 1509 so that the Spanish were permitted to eat meat, eggs, and dairy on certain prohibited days. The town of Meco, Spain, obtained a bull from Pope Innocent VIII in the late 15th century exempting its 14,000 inhabitants from fast and abstinence, even on Good Friday, owing to their alleged large distance from the sea.

The one who originally obtained this dispensation was Íñigo López de Mendoza y Quiñones, the second Count of Tendilla and Lord of Meco. He requested the papal bull, and many say that the Vatican's favorable decision was granted in recognition of the services López de Mendoza had rendered to Pope Innocent VIII and the Roman Court since Meco is not the farthest Spanish town from the sea.[80]

All these bulls stemmed from the contributions which the Spanish made to advance the Faith against the Church's enemies through the Crusades. As such, some Spanish missals will list reduced days of fasting and abstinence with the notation "con Bula de Cruzada."

One of the final Crusade Bulls issued was that issued to Alphonsus XIII by Pope Leo XIII in 1902 which was in force for 12 years. Father Slater writes on this bull:

> Besides plenary and other indulgences, this Bull grants to the faithful laity who live in the Spanish dominions, or who come thither from elsewhere, the faculty of eating meat on fasting-days, but this faculty can only be used within the Spanish dominions.[81]

The Bull of the Crusade was ultimately extinguished on December 31, 1914, by Pope Benedict XV, who replaced it with the Pontifical Indults, whose proceeds were used for the founding and maintenance of seminaries. The fasting and abstinence pardons were later extinguished in 1966 with the issuance of *Poenitemini*.

Fasting in the New World

Fasting and abstinence, along with Holy Days of Obligation, were, in practice, highly varied depending on each nation and territory. We see this liturgical diversity in the various colonies.

For instance, Catholics in the colonies in Florida and Louisiana observed these fasting days:

> The fasting days were all days in Lent; the Ember days; the eves of Christmas, Candlemas, Annunciation, Assumption, All Saints, the feasts of the Apostles except St Philip and St James and St John, and the Nativity of St John the Baptist; all Fridays except within twelve days of Christmas and between Easter and Ascension, and the eve of Ascension.[82]

For abstinence from meat, they would have observed:

> All Sundays in Lent, all Saturdays throughout the year, Monday and Tuesday before Ascension, and St Mark's day were of abstinence from flesh meat.[83]

The western colonies under Spanish rule in modern day Texas, New Mexico, Arizona, and California observed as fast days:

> ...all days in Lent except Sunday; eves of Christmas, Whit Sunday, St Mathias, St John the Baptist, St Peter and St Paul, St James, St Lawrence, Assumption, St Bartholomew, St Matthew, St Simon and St Jude, All Saints, St Andrew, and St Thomas.[84]

There was a distinction made between Natives (i.e., Indios) and European settlers. The papal bull *"Altitudo Divini Concilii"* of Pope Paul III in 1537 reduced the days of penance and those of hearing Mass for the Indians out of pastoral concern due to the physically demanding lifestyle that they lived and largely because they fasted so much already. As a result, the only fasting days required under pain of sin for the Native Americans were the Fridays in Lent, Holy Saturday, and Christmas Eve. Pope Paul III also dispensed them from the precept of abstaining from dairy, egg, and flesh meat on certain days as well.

Importantly, those aided by these significantly reduced days included not only the tribes which inhabited the modern-day United States but natives of islands as far as the Philippines as the author of *Dei Praesidio Suffulus* notes:

> The lands discovered by the Spaniards and the Portuguese were collectively called the Indies: divided into the East Indies and the West Indies. There are differing positions on where

these two Indies were delimited, but the official division comes from Gregory XIII who declared on 11 October 1579 *vivæ vocis oraculo* that the East Indies encompassed the lands of Mauritania eastwards, which belonged to the King of Portugal. Benedict XIV, however, in the bull *Indiarum gentibus*, promulgated on 24 February 1748, modified the boundaries so that the East Indies now encompassed the lands from the Cape of Good Hope until the realms of Japan and China.

Gregory XIII, in the same declaration of 1579, denoted the West Indies as encompassing the lands from the Canaries westwards, belonging to either the King of Spain or the King of Portugal. The bull of Urban VIII, *Alias felicis*, promulgated on 20 December 1631, simply repeated the declaration of Gregory XIII and, therefore, did not shift the delimitations of the West Indies. The Philippine Islands, long known to Spain as the Islands of the West (in Spanish, Islas del Poniente), as well as Japan, came within the circumscription of the West Indies, by virtue of the bull *Onerosa pastoralis officii cura,* promulgated by Clement VIII on 12 December 1600.[85]

The discovery of the New World also brought with it questions directly impacting what may or may not be consumed on days of fasting and one of the most significant of those concerned a newly discovered substance – chocolate. Was chocolate a liquid or a solid? Could someone consume it on a day of fasting at any time since it is a liquid when heated and left at room temperature? *The Economics of Chocolate* describes this interesting history:

The first fight over the definition of 'chocolate' was within the Catholic Church. After the Spanish conquest of America, chocolate was imported to Europe and consumed as a beverage. In the sixteenth and seventeenth centuries in Catholic countries such as Spain, France, or Italy, the issue of whether or not it was permitted to drink chocolate during Christian fasting periods...arose. Christian fasting implied that flesh is 'mortified,' therefore more 'nourishing' substances couldn't be taken. If chocolate was a drink, it did not break the fast, but if it was a food, then it could not be consumed during Christian fasting periods...

Catholic scholars debated the issue. Juan de Cardenas (1591 – 1913) and Nicephoro Sebasto Melisseno (1665) argued that chocolate could not be consumed during the fast because of the addition of butter. Antonio de Escobar y Mendoza (1626), Antonio de Leon Pinelo (1636), and Tomas Hurtado (1645) had a different opinion. According to them, it depended if (and how much) nourishing substances were added to the chocolate. If mixed with water it became a drink and was thus permitted (as was wine), but if mixed with other substances (as milk, eggs, and dry bread) – it became a food and, therefore, was forbidden. Cardinal Francesco Mario Brancaccio (1664) also argued if the water component prevailed over the cocoa component, then chocolate did not break the fast...

Several popes were asked to settle the dispute as leaders of the Catholic Church. According to Coe and Coe (2013), Popes Gregory XIII, Clement VII, Paul V, Pius V, Urban VIII, Clement XI, and Benedict XIV all agreed in private that chocolate did not break the fast. However, there was never an official Papal statement to end the debate.[86]

Peter Dens in *A Synopsis of the Moral Theology* presents the chocolate conundrum in a more succinct manner:

Does the taking of chocolate break an ecclesiastical fast? It is certain, with the consent of all, that to eat chocolate undiluted breaks the fast; because it is food and is taken by way of food. The question is concerning the drinking of chocolate; to wit, when chocolate, mixed with water and diluted and boiled, is drunk, or rather, is sucked. Cozza and La Croix propose this as a question controverted by their patrons on both sides, whom they cite. Benedict XIV, the Supreme Pontiff, has published a lucid dissertation upon this question, who, however, resolves that it is more safe to abstain from chocolate on a fast day; and to him we adhere with Billuart. The reason is, because such a potion in itself, and more especially serves for nourishment, and not properly cooling, or for quenching thirst; for it is a kind of hot concoction. This is confirmed from the fact that by this potion weak persons are nourished.[87]

To a serious Catholic, what was and was not permitted on a day of fasting was worth careful consideration.

Lenten Fast is Altered

As previously mentioned, the Lenten fast was originally observed as a single meal taken after sunset. By the 9th century, a small collation in the evening was introduced on account of the physical work done by the Benedictine monks. It eventually was permitted to all classes of people and not just monks. And the one meal was moved to 3 o'clock from sunset.

By the fourteenth century, the meal had begun to move up steadily until it began to take place even at 12 o'clock. The change became so common it became part of the Church's discipline. In one interesting but often unknown fact, because the monks would pray the liturgical hour of None before they would eat their meal, the custom of calling midday by the name of "noon" entered our vocabulary. 12 PM is noon because of Catholic fasting. The collation remained in the evening.

The Protestant Attack on Penance

In the Middle Ages, abstinence from meat on Fridays and during Lent was not only Church law – it was civil law as well. And people gladly obeyed these laws out of respect for the teaching authority of the Church. Yet after the Protestant revolt which began in 1517 and continued through the middle of the 1600s, this was to change. Zwingli, the protestant leader from Switzerland, directed multiple attacks against the merits of good works, including fasting and abstinence through the infamous "The Affair of Sausage" in 1522. He audaciously claimed that since Scripture was the only authority, sausages should be eaten publicly in Lent in defiance.[88]

The same occurred in England, which followed the revolt of Luther and his peers. King Henry VIII, who was previously given the title "Defender of the Faith" by Pope Leo X for his defense against Luther, succumbed to heresy and schism when he broke from the Lord's established Church on earth in 1533 to engage in adultery. Church property was seized. Catholics were killed. Catholicism was made illegal in England in 1559 under Queen Elizabeth I, and for 232 years, except during the brief reign of the Catholic King James II (1685 – 1688), the Catholic Mass was illegal until 1791. Yet the Anglicans at least kept the Catholic customs of abstinence for some years.

English Royalty proclamations supporting abstinence of meat continued to occur in England in 1563, 1619, 1625, 1627, and 1631. The same likewise occurred in 1687 under King James II. After the Revolution in 1688 and the overthrow of Catholicism by William III and Mary II, the laws were no longer enforced and in 1863 were officially expunged by the Statute Law Revision Act . Similar changes occurred throughout Europe as Protestants reviled the fast.

Protestants largely abandoned fasting and other forms of mortification altogether in a complete rupture with the practice of all of Christianity back to the Apostles themselves. While some Lutherans and Methodists will voluntarily keep fasting days, it is uncommon and not practiced under obligation. Methodists, who were founded by John Wesley in the 18th century, for instance, if they do fast, are more likely to observe the "Daniel Fast" during the season of Lent, which is categorized by abstinence from "meat, fish, egg, dairy products, chocolates, ice creams, sugar, sweets, wine or any alcoholic beverages" as taken from the Book of Daniel 10:3.

By the 1900s, the Episcopalian Church, the American branch of Anglicanism, largely abandoned all fasting and abstinence by re-writing their Book of Common Prayer (BCP):

> The 1928 BCP in its table of fasts listed 'other days of fasting on which the Church requires such a measure of abstinence as is more especially suited to extraordinary acts and

exercises of devotion.' These included the forty days of Lent, the Ember Days, and Fridays. No distinction was made between fasting and abstinence. The 1979 BCP dropped the Ember Days from the list and refers to both Lenten weekdays and Fridays outside of the Christmas and Easter seasons as Days of Special Devotion 'observed by special acts of discipline and self-denial' (p. 17). While this permits the traditional observance of Days of Abstinence, it clearly leaves the nature of the special acts of discipline and self-denial to the individual.[89]

Even amid the Protestant revolt, weakening discipline continued even in Catholic nations. As previously stated, the twice weekly fast on Wednesday and Friday goes back to the Apostles. In Ireland for instance the use of meat on all Wednesdays of the year was prohibited until around the middle of the 17th century.[90] This harkened back to the vestige of those earlier times when Wednesdays were days of weekly fasting as Father Slater notes in "A Short History of Moral Theology" published in 1909:

> The obligation of fasting on all Wednesdays and Fridays ceased almost entirely about the tenth century, but the fixing of those days by ecclesiastical authority for fasting, and the desire to substitute a Christian observance at Rome for certain pagan rites celebrated in connection with the seasons of the year, seem to have given rise to our Ember Days... About the tenth century the obligation of the Friday fast was reduced to one of abstinence from flesh meat, and the Wednesday fast after being similarly mitigated gradually disappeared altogether.[91]

The Sacrifice of St. John of the Cross for the Monastic Fast

We can trace the roots of the monastic fast through Chapter 41 of the Rule of St. Benedict which dates to approximately 515 AD. While the entirety of a monk's life was one of moderation in food and in drink, the monastic fast added additional self-denial starting on September 14th, the Feast of the Exaltation of the Holy Cross, and continuing until Ash Wednesday. When Ash Wednesday arrived, the monk would then follow the stricter Lenten fast. As a result, over half the year of a monk's life would be spent in fasting.

The monastic fast and the Divine Office governed the monk's life. In fact, the only part of the year in which the monk was to eat two meals each day was from Easter to Pentecost! Chapter 41 of the Rule of St. Benedict states:

> From holy Easter to Pentecost, the brothers eat at noon and take supper in the evening. Beginning with Pentecost and continuing throughout the summer, the monks fast until mid-afternoon on Wednesday and Friday, unless they are working in the fields or the summer heat is oppressive. On the other days they eat dinner at noon. Indeed, the abbot may decide that they should continue to eat dinner at noon every day if they have work in the fields or if the summer heat remains extreme. Similarly, he should so regulate and arrange all matters that souls may be saved, and the brothers may go about their activities without justifiable grumbling. From the thirteenth of September to the beginning of Lent, they always take their meal in mid-afternoon. Finally, from the beginning of Lent to Easter, they eat towards evening. Let Vespers be

celebrated early enough so that there is no need for a lamp while eating, and that everything can be finished by daylight. Indeed, at all times let supper or the hour of the fast-day meal be so scheduled that everything can be done by daylight.[92]

The monastic fast was at the heart of the reforms of St. John of the Cross for the Carmelite Order. At the age of 21, St. John entered the Carmelite Order by a prompting from the Holy Ghost on February 24, 1563. At that time, he took the name John of St. Mathias since he received the habit on the Feast of St. Mathias. At the onset, St. John felt called to personally keep the ancient Rule of the Carmelites that was given by St. Albert, Patriarch of Jerusalem, which was approved by Pope Innocent IV in 1254. His superiors permitted him to do so. However, the Carmelites at that time instead kept a mitigated rule which had been approved by Pope Eugenius IV in 1447. The mitigated rule allowed the consumption of meat, and it did not require the fast that lasted from the Feast of the Holy Cross all the way to Easter. It also permitted the friars to wear shoes.

Yet, St. John was called by God to observe the ancient Rule. He did so while at the Carmelite Monastery, even though this brought the ridicule of his brethren down upon him. Many days he would go hungry as there were no special meals prepared for him. Yet, he continued to observe the ancient observance and would permit himself no excuse from any function at the monastery.

At the age of 25, St. John was asked to prepare for the priesthood even though he felt far too unworthy to do so. Yet, he submitted and was ordained; his whole life he submitted to his superiors. Feeling unworthy to offer the Holy Sacrifice, St. John prayed at his first Mass to persevere in purity his whole life. God answered Him at that Mass through a voice which said, "Thy prayer is granted."[93]

The young St. John felt drawn to the Carthusian Order, but he was asked by St. Teresa of Avila to help her in the restoration of the primitive Carmelite Rule of Life. He agreed and received the habit of the primitive Order. Along with two other friars in 1568, Saint John renewed his solemn vows and renounced the mitigations of the rule sanctioned by Pope Eugenius IV. And they promised both Our Lord and Our Lady that they would live under the Primitive Rule until death. In keeping with the custom St. Teresa established for the sisters to change their names to avoid all connection with their family names, the saint changed his name to John of the Cross.

During the years that followed, again with the support of his superiors, St. John founded many monasteries. These religious observed the stricter 'discalced' rule with the approval of the Order. St. John chose to live as one that was abject and completely impoverished. Within it, he chose the poorest and smallest room for himself. He had the gift of 'reading souls' and counseled many nuns and friars. It was during this time that he received many mystical experiences, including trances and visions while in prayer or saying Holy Mass.

It is well documented that on several occasions St. John performed exorcisms to relieve the possessed. In one of the better-known incidents, he freed a nun from the devil whom many learned theologians at the famed University of Salamanca mistakenly thought to be exceptionally wise and prophetic. St. John discerned the presence of the evil one because the nun refused to say the Creed correctly. He then began the process of exorcism by insisting that she learn the basics of the catechism well. This incident helps show us how important it is for all confirmed Catholics to study and know the catechism well. Moreover, it illuminates one of the most overlooked aspects of studying the Faith, namely that it is a powerful protection against the attacks of the infernal demons.

After nine years of his keeping the Primitive Rule, St. John was forcibly arrested by the Carmelite Order which wished to suppress the Primitive Rule. St. John underwent severe punishment as a prisoner in a Carmelite monastery. There, the prior treated him with great irreverence, forbade him to say Mass, starved him, and refused to let him change his habit or bathe for the entire nine months of his imprisonment. The monks even employed mental abuse by whispering all kinds of untruths outside the door of his cell; for example, that the monasteries he helped found had been destroyed by ecclesial authorities.

St. John was treated with the utmost contempt, but he welcomed it all in a spirit of penance and making reparation. He longed to suffer and was most docile and patient of suffering. By the accounts that were written, the patient endurance of his unjust torture resembled the patience of Our Lord in His Passion. After nearly a year, he received a vision from Our Lady with the means to escape; and he did so.

He spent the remaining years of his life in constant prayer while working for the Order. He served as Vicar-Provincial, he performed miracles, and he continued to found monasteries that followed the primitive Rule. This lasted for many years, and then in 1587 Pope Sixtus V sanctioned the separation of the friars of the reform from the friars of the mitigation. At last, in 1588 the first General Chapter of the Reform was held where St. John of the Cross was made the first Consultor and Prior of Segovia.

Around this time, he was in deep prayer when Our Lord spoke to Him in a vision and asked, "John, what shall I give thee for all thou hast done and suffered for Me?" And after He asked three times, St. John responded, "To suffer and to be held in contempt for Thy sake." And his prayer was granted.

In the ensuing years, he was relieved of all offices as superior, he spent his remaining years under a superior who was unkind and hateful towards him for having corrected a fault of his years before, and he died in humiliation. But St. John endured it all and desired the physical and spiritual torment he endured all for the graces it brought and for the sake of God. At last, he died in December 1591 on a Saturday, the day dedicated to Our Lady, which was revealed to Him.

Miraculously, his body and his bandages gave forth a great perfume whose smell could not be contained. Great light filled his tomb just days after he died, and his body was incorrupt. It was determined that some of his limbs were to go to some of the houses of the Order, so it was divided up. And the relics of his body brought many miracles to those who touched them.

St. Francis of Paolo and the Beer Fast of Monks

Around this same era, St. Francis of Paola was born in 1416 to parents who were childless for many years. Yet the parents pleaded through the intercession of St. Francis of Assisi that they should be given children by God. And so, their prayers were heard. They had three children.

As a young boy, St. Francis journeyed on a pilgrimage to Rome and Assisi and decided to follow the will of God and become a hermit. Before he was even 20 years old, he began to attract followers and thus founded the Hermits of Saint Francis of Assisi, who were approved by the Holy See in 1474. In 1492 they were renamed as the Franciscan Order of Minim Friars. The use of "Minim" meant that they counted themselves as the least worthy of those in the household of God.

St. Francis was regarded as a miracle worker, prophet, and defender of the poor. In 1464 St. Francis wanted to cross the Straits of Messina to reach Sicily, but a boatman refused to take him. St. Francis responded by laying his cloak on the water, tying one end to his staff to make a sail, and then he proceeded to sail across with his companions. Franz Liszt wrote a piece of music inspired by the incident.

At the request of Pope Sixtus IV, he traveled to Paris and helped Louis XI prepare for death. He also used his position to help restore peace between France and Brittany by advising a marriage between the ruling families and between France and Spain by persuading Louis XI to return some disputed land. St. Francis had a love for animals and took a vow to never eat any animals, even fish. According to his biographers, it is said:

> Francis had a favorite trout that he called 'Antonella.' One day, one of the priests, who provided religious services, saw the trout swimming about in his pool. To him it was just a delicious dish, so he caught it and took it home, tossing it into the frying pan. Francis missed 'Antonella' and realized what had happened. He asked one of his followers to go to the priest to get it back. The priest, annoyed by this great concern for a mere fish, threw the cooked trout on the ground, shattering it into several pieces. The hermit sent by Francis gathered up the broken pieces in his hands and brought them back to Francis. Francis placed the pieces back in the pool and, looking up to Heaven and praying, said: 'Antonella, in the name of Charity, return to life.' The trout immediately became whole and swam joyously around his pool as if nothing had happened. The friars and the workers who witnessed this miracle were deeply impressed by the miracle.[94]

St. Francis also raised his pet lamb from the dead after it had been killed and eaten by workmen:

> Being in need of food, the workmen caught and slaughtered Francis' pet lamb, Martinello, roasting it in their lime kiln. They were eating when the Saint approached them, looking for the lamb. They told him they had eaten it, having no other food. He asked what they had done with the fleece and the bones. They told him they had thrown them into the furnace. Francis walked over to the furnace, looked into the fire and called 'Martinello, come out!' The lamb jumped out, completely untouched, bleating happily on seeing his master.[95]

St. Francis of Paola died on Good Friday, April 2, 1507, in Pelssis, France as the Passion according to St. John was read to him. He was canonized in 1519 by Pope Leo X. Tragically, in 1562 Protestant Huguenots broke open his tomb, found his body incorrupt, and burned it; the bones were salvaged by Catholics, and distributed as relics to various churches.

Concerning fasting, it was his order, the Minims, who began the "beer fast" of the monks. George Ryan, writing for *uCatholic*, explains:

> In the early 1600s, Paulaner friars of the Order of Minims moved from Southern Italy and settled in the monastery Neudeck ob der Au in Bavaria. The friars observed a strict ascetic lifestyle, living in perpetual abstinence from all meat and dairy products. This 'Lenten way of life,' termed vita *quadragesimalis* in Latin, is a distinct character of the Order of Minims. Because they already observed a Lenten lifestyle year-round, they invented a beer only

diet for Lent as a special fast beyond what they already observed.

In 1634, the Paulaner friars came up with a special brew, so malty and rich they could sustain themselves on it alone for the entire 40 days of Lent. The 'liquid bread' as they called it, was full of carbohydrates and other nutrients, with the idea being that liquids cleanse both body and soul. It was a common belief that the more 'liquid bread' one consumed, the more purified they would be for Lent.

The doppelback, as it is called in German, was quite strong for its time, and people occasionally got drunk off it. When the friar's recipe improved, they feared the beer was too tasty and intoxicating to be drunk during Lent.

Around the year 1700, they sent a barrel to the pope asking for his opinion. However, on its travels through the Alps and through the hot Italian sun, it went foul, and the pope received a flagrant concoction that resembled nothing of the original brew. After tasting it, the pope sent a message that the disgusting liquid would most definitely help cleanse the friars of their sins, and so the Order of Minim's tradition of leitenbock was born: 40 days without solid food, drinking only water and beer.[96]

Even today, some people strive to voluntarily observe a Lenten period with no solid food and only beverages like doppelbock in imitation of the Minims.[97]

The Example of St. Charles Borromeo

Around this same time, it was the saintly archbishop, St. Charles Borromeo (1538 – 1584), the hero of the Counter Reformation against the Protestants, who championed fasting and penance in northern Italy.

Rogation Days have been observed for centuries even if the Catholic Church in our modern era has virtually forgotten them. A similar situation occurred before in the Diocese of Milan. It was St. Charles who restored them and enhanced them in that Diocese. Interestingly, even though Rome never mandated fasting on the Rogation Days, since they occur during the Easter Season, St. Charles Borromeo mandated them in his own diocese.

Dom Guéranger in the Liturgical Year provides us with a holy example which should show us the spirit of penance which should animate all our lives on the Rogation Days:

> St. Charles Borromeo, who restored in his diocese of Milan so many ancient practices of

piety, was sure not to be indifferent about the Rogation days. He spared neither word nor example to reanimate this salutary devotion among his people. He ordered fasting to be observed during these three days; he fasted himself on bread and water. The procession, in which all the clergy of the city were obliged to join, and which began after the sprinkling of ashes, started from the cathedral at an early hour in the morning, and was not over till three or four o'clock in the afternoon. Thirteen churches were visited on the Monday; nine, on the Tuesday; and eleven, on the Wednesday. The saintly archbishop celebrated Mass and preached in one of these churches.[98]

St. Charles Borromeo did not only encourage the Rogation Days. He ministered personally to thousands of plague-stricken victims when the civil authorities had fled Milan. He offered Masses, administered the Sacraments, consistently led processions, and offered an authentic Catholic response to a pandemic.[99]

In this same period, the fast of Advent, which had continued to decline, had taken the form of only Wednesday and Friday penance. To stir the people to observe the true spirit of penance, even beyond the letter of the law, St. Charles also strongly urged those in Milan to fast on the Monday, Wednesday, and Friday of each week of Advent.[100] In one key distinction, Milan keeps the Ambrosian Rite, which differs in several aspects from the Roman Rite. One of those key differences is that Advent in the Ambrosian Rite always begins on the Sunday after the feast of Saint Martin of Tours, alluding back centuries before to St. Martin's Lent as it was practiced in the Roman Rite.

Lenten Fast is Dramatically Changed in 1741

By the Early Modern Era, the Church mandated three primary categories of fasts: the Lenten fast, the Ember Days, and the Vigils of certain feasts. Likewise, to these both Friday and Saturday abstinence was observed as the 1649 Douay Catechism affirms. Some of the most significant changes to fasting would occur under the reign of Pope Benedict XIV who reigned from 1740 – 1758.

On May 31, 1741, Pope Benedict XIV issued *Non Ambiginius* which granted permission to eat meat on some fasting days, while at the same time explicitly forbidding the consumption of both fish and flesh meat at the same meal on all fasting days during the year and on the Sundays of Lent. Beforehand, the forty days of Lent were always held as days of complete abstinence from meat. For the first time, meat could be consumed during Lent. This is the origin of "partial abstinence," even though the term would not appear until the 1917 Code of Canon Law. Yet even with these changes, Pope Benedict XIV implored the faithful to return to the devotion of earlier eras:

> The observance of Lent is the very badge of the Christian warfare. By it we prove ourselves not to be enemies of the cross of Christ. By it we avert the scourges of divine justice. By it we gain strength against the princes of darkness, for it shields us with heavenly help. Should mankind grow remiss in their observance of Lent, it would be a detriment to God's glory, a disgrace to the Catholic religion, and a danger to Christian souls. Neither can it be doubted that such negligence would become the source of misery to the world, of public calamity, and of private woe.

Yet, despite this admonition, changes continued during the 18th and 19th centuries as Father Antoine Villien's *History of the Commandments* from 1915 documents:

> The use of meat on Sundays [of Lent] was at first tolerated, then expressly permitted, for the greater part of Lent. Old people still remember the time when its use was completely forbidden in France from the Friday of Passion week to Easter. Later, new dispensations allowed the gradual extension of the Sunday privilege to Tuesday and Thursday of each week, up to Thursday before Palm Sunday. About the beginning of the pontificate of Pius IX [c. 1846], Monday was added to the days on which abstinence need not be observed; a few years later the use of meat on those four days began to be permitted up to Wednesday of Holy Week. Lastly the Saturdays, except Ember Saturday and Holy Saturday, were included in the dispensations.[101]

As seen with the gradual change to abstinence days regarding lacticinia and eggs, some changes occurred as well with items like lard. One of those first changes was under Pope Pius IX who granted to the faithful in England the ability to use lard and meat drippings as condiments on all fasting and abstinence days except for Good Friday. This rescript of May 19, 1860, applied to the meal as well as to the collation (i.e., the evening snack permitted on a fasting day).[102]

The Definition of Meat Changes

Part of the attack on the patrimony of fasting and abstinence took the form of dispensations permitting certain animals to be eaten on account of such animals spending most of their time in water. Even though these animals were not cold-blooded, like fish, the faithful received permission in some places to eat animals like the capybara, the largest rodent in the world, in addition to beaver and muskrat.

For instance, Father Sojo, a Venezuelan priest, is said in "Fauna de Venezuela y su conservación" to have gone to Italy at the end of the eighteenth century and obtained a papal bull approving the consumption of capybara for Lent on account of its amphibious habits. Prussian naturalist Alexander von Humboldt wrote on capybara meat during his visit to Venezuela in the early 1800s: "The missionary monks do not hesitate to eat these hams during Lent. According to their zoological classification they place the armadillo, the thick-nosed tapir, and the manatee, near the tortoises; the first, because it is covered with a hard armor like a sort of shell; and the others because they are amphibious."[103]

Likewise, in the 17th century, theologians in Paris turned their minds to a question posed by Archbishop Francois de Laval, the first bishop of Quebec, who asked whether it was permissible to eat beaver meat during Lent. The ruling from Paris was "Yes" for the same reason that capybara was permitted.

An 1850 issue of The Dublin University Magazine also states that beaver tail was customarily eaten during Lent by the "strict churchmen of Northern Germany," while the Canadian Journal of Industry, Science and Art writes:

> [A] Dutch writer, states that the animal was used as food in Holland, in the time of the Crusades ; and he repeats the common notice, that its tail and paws were eaten as fish, with a safe conscience, during the religious fasts but the monks of a convent of Chartreux, at Villeneuve-les-Avignon, seem to have carried this indulgent notion farther and to have

accounted their entire carcass among the 'mets maigres.'[104]

Yet the author adds that St. Albert the Great "says that the whole flesh was abominable, except the tail." Historians also cite this exception, along with the fur trade, as the reason why the beaver population of North America was so decimated by hunters.

This continued a trend that originated in the post-Renaissance period that also saw the permission of puffin on days of abstinence. In 1698 the St. Michael's Benedictine Abbey in Le Tréport began to eat puffin, a seagoing bird, on days of abstinence. While the Archbishop of Rouen initially condemned such a practice, he later overturned his decision and permitted the bird to be eaten on days of abstinence after an examination by the medical college in Rouen found that puffins spent most of their time at sea.[105]

Even in current times, a 2002 document from the Archdiocese of Detroit stated that "there is a long-standing permission to permit the consumption of muskrat on days of abstinence, including Fridays of Lent." Tradition has it that the pastor of St. Anne Parish in Detroit, Fr. Gabriel Richard, lobbied for the original dispensation for eating muskrat for southeastern Michigan Catholics during the early 1800s. Detroit Catholic states:

> Historical sources from the early 1800s attest to the fact that local residents were sometimes in a state of starvation, eating chopped hay for sustenance and appealing to the government for federal funds to purchase flour. Often the only food left to consume was the meat of livestock, roaming deer, or the numerous muskrats lingering along the riverbanks.[106]

And thus, dispensation was granted.

American Fasting & Abstinence Weaken throughout the 1800s

In addition to regional dispensations, sweeping changes also occurred for all Catholics early in America's history. At the time of America's founding, the fast days observed by the new Republic consisted of the Ember Days; the forty days Lent; Wednesdays and Fridays in Advent; and the vigils of Christmas, Whitsun Sunday (i.e., Pentecost), Saints Peter and Paul, and All Saints. Abstinence was practiced on all Fridays and Saturdays of the year unless a Holy Day of Obligation were to occur on them.

The Third Provincial Council of Baltimore in 1837, with approval of Pope Gregory XVI, began to reduce these practices. The Council dispensed from fast and abstinence the Wednesdays of Advent, except for the Ember Wednesday in Advent.

At this time, complete abstinence was still observed on all Saturdays but over the course of the 19th century, the dispensations from Saturday abstinence became universal. Mara Morrow, author of *Sin in the Sixties*, summarizes these changes:

> In 1840 the Fourth Provincial Council of Baltimore asked for a perpetual renewal of an indult dispensing from abstinence on Saturdays, and this indult was renewed for twenty years by Pope Gregory XVI. In 1866, the Second Plenary Council asked that all dispensations granted to the diocese of Baltimore be extended to other American dioceses, but Pope Pius IX preferred individual requests from each bishop in the United States.

In 1884, the U.S. bishops who were meeting at the Third Plenary Council decided it would be difficult to pass uniform legislation on the subject of fast and abstinence and hence left it to the authority of provincial councils to determine what was best for their territories. Leo XIII in 1886 granted U.S. bishops the authority to dispense each year from abstinence on Saturdays.[107]

Similarly, Pope Gregory XVI in a rescript from June 28, 1831, granted a dispensation to all Catholics of Scotland from abstinence on Saturdays throughout the year, except on Saturdays that were also days of fasting. Dispensations were granted in many nations, illustrating a weakening in discipline not only in America.

With the growing number of Irish immigrants to America in the early 1800s, special attention was given to dispense from the law of abstinence when St. Patricks' Day fell on a Friday. This was done for the members of the Charitable Irish Society of Boston in 1837 and would become customary in the United States.

Christmastide Exceptions for Saturday Abstinence

For those Catholics who wish to keep Saturday abstinence in honor of Our Lady's request for penance, how should we model our Saturday abstinence? In short, we should keep the teaching of Pope Gregory VII (reigned 1073 - 1085) who declared that the exceptions to Saturday abstinence were major solemnities, which would seem to include both Holy Days of Obligation and great feasts, such as those which used to be among the 36 Holy Days of Obligation in past times. This list comes from the papal bull "Universa Per Orbem" which altered the required Holy Days of Obligation for the Universal Church to consist of 35 such days:

1. Nativity of Our Lord
2. Circumcision of Our Lord
3. Epiphany of Our Lord
4. Monday within the Octave of the Resurrection
5. Tuesday within the Octave of the Resurrection
6. Ascension
7. Monday within the Octave of Pentecost
8. Tuesday within the Octave of Pentecost
9. Most Holy Trinity
10. Corpus Christi
11. Finding of the Holy Cross (May 3)
12. Purification of the Blessed Virgin Mary
13. Annunciation of the Blessed Virgin Mary
14. Assumption of the Blessed Virgin Mary
15. Nativity of the Blessed Virgin Mary
16. Dedication of St. Michael
17. Nativity of St. John the Baptist
18. SS. Peter and Paul
19. St. Andrew
20. St. James
21. St. John (the December feast day)
22. St. Thomas
23. SS. Philip and James
24. St. Bartholomew
25. St. Matthew
26. SS. Simon and Jude
27. St. Matthias
28. St. Stephen the First Martyr (the December feast day)
29. The Holy Innocents
30. St. Lawrence
31. St. Sylvester
32. St. Joseph
33. St. Anne
34. All Saints
35. Principle Patrons of One's Country, City, etc.

Additionally, if we model our Saturday abstinence based on our forefathers in the Faith, one of the few exceptions to Saturday fasting - in places that maintained this as law - was the Saturdays (but never Fridays) of Christmastide (i.e., December 25th through February 2nd). France had such an exception as the Catechism of Perseverance makes mention:

> In France, the law of abstinence on Saturday became general. There was no exception, save in some dioceses for the Saturdays between Christmas and the Purification. Hitherto, Spain has introduced no modifications as regards the liberty of eating meat on Saturday beyond this, that the intestines and extremities of animals may be used. The abstinence of Saturday, though less general than that of Friday, should not be less religiously observed. The authority that prescribed both is the same: the authority of our holy Mother the Church, of whom the Savior Himself said, If any one will not obey the Church, let him be to you as the heathen and the publican.[108]

Such an exception also existed in at least some Dioceses of the United States before the dispensation from year-round Saturday abstinence - vigils, Lent, and ember days excepting - that began in the mid-1830s and continued until its complete abrogation by the 1917 Code. The 1822 Laity's Directory for New York mentions this exception.[109]

Pope Leo XIII Continues the Relaxation of Discipline

Throughout the centuries covered thus far, Lenten abstinence included not only abstinence from meat but also generally from eggs and dairy products, though exceptions were granted in various localities.

In 1886 Leo XIII allowed meat, eggs, and milk products on Sundays of Lent and at the main meal on every weekday [of Lent] except Wednesday and Friday in the [United States]. Holy Saturday was not included in the dispensation. A small piece of bread was permitted in the morning with coffee, tea, chocolate, or a similar beverage.

While the evening collation had been widespread since the 14th century, the practice of an additional morning snack (i.e., a frustulum) was widely introduced only around the 18th century as part of the gradual relaxation of discipline. Volume 12 of *The Jurist*, published by the Catholic University of America in 1952, writes, "It is stated that the two-ounce breakfast arose at the time of St. Alphonsus, since which time the usage of the popular two and eight-ounce standards for the breakfast and the collation, respectively, has been extant."[110]

Mara Morrow in *Sin in the Sixties* elaborates on the concessions given by Pope Leo XIII which in the late 19th century expanded the practice of the frustulum and further reduced strict abstinence:

> It also allowed for the use of eggs and milk products at the evening collation daily during Lent and at the principal meal when meat was not allowed. [It] further allowed a small piece of bread in the morning with a beverage, the possibility of taking the principal meal at noon or in the evening, and the use of lard and meat drippings in the preparation of foods. Those exempt from the law of fasting were permitted to eat meat, eggs, and milk more than once a day.[111]

Consequently, *The Baltimore Manual* published by the Third Plenary Council of Baltimore in 1884 states: "Only one full meal is allowed, to be taken about noon or later. Besides this full meal, a collation of eight ounces is allowed. If the full meal is taken about the middle of the day, the collation will naturally be taken in the evening; if the full meal is taken late in the day, the collation may be taken at noon. Besides the full meal and collation, the general custom has made it lawful to take up to two ounces of bread (without butter) and a cup of some warm liquid – as coffee or tea – in the morning. This is important to observe, for by means of this many persons are enabled – and therefore obliged – to keep the fast who could not otherwise do so."[112]

The Catechism of Father Patrick Powers published in Ireland in 1905 mentions that Lenten abstinence includes flesh meat and "anything produced from animals, as milk, butter, cheese, eggs." However, Father Patrick notes, "In some countries, however, milk is allowed at collation." The United States was one of those nations whereas Ireland and others were not granted such dispensations. The use of eggs and milk during Lent would change drastically in a few years with the 1917 Code of Canon Law. The 1905 Lenten regulations for the Archdiocese of Toronto also added the encouragement: "The faithful are recommended during Lent to abstain from all intoxicating drinks in remembrance of the Sacred Thirst of Our Lord on the Cross."[113]

In 1895, the workingmen's privilege gave bishops in the United States the ability to permit meat in some circumstances. Mara Morrow summarizes that these circumstances occurred when there was "difficulty in observing the common law of abstinence, excluding Fridays, Ash Wednesday, Holy Week, and the Vigil of Christmas. This workingmen's privilege (or indult) allowed only for meat once a day during Lent, taken at the principal meal, and never taken in conjunction with fish. This indult was extended not only to the laborer but to his family, as well. The motivation of such an indult was no doubt to allow for enough sustenance such that the many Catholic immigrants to the United States who worked as manual laborers could perform their difficult, energy-demanding physical work without danger to their health."[114]

Fasting Wanes in Rome

Fasting days were also slowly reduced in Rome as well. By 1893, the only fasting days kept in Rome were the forty days of Lent, the Ember Days, and the Vigils of the Purification, of Pentecost, of St. John the Baptist, of Ss. Peter and Paul, of the Assumption, of All Saints, and of Christmas.[115] In just a few years, Rome would abrogate the fast on the Vigil of the Purification and of St. John the Baptist.

Fasting's Decline in the Philippines

America's decline in fasting is not the only example of a progressive relaxation of discipline. The collapse of a robust life of fasting and abstinence by Filipino Catholics also preceded the 20th century.

While Pope Paul III had decreed in 1537 that the indios were bound to a substantially smaller number of fasting and abstinence days, it was not until March 3, 1852, that the Holy See decreed such exceptions would apply equally to mestizos. The term "mestizo" referred to someone who was born of a European father or mother and a native mother or father. The rescript referred only to those who were equally half Indio and half European, and thus, the exception did not apply to those whose parents were European and mestizo. Hence, fasting rules in the Philippines differed between indios, mestizos, and all others (e.g., pureblood Spaniards born in Spain but domiciled in the Philippines, pureblood Spaniards born in the Philippines, and Europeans not subject to the Spanish Crown residing in the Philippines).

Why the distinction? The indios were regarded as poor members of society and, even if they did happen to be landowners or first-order mestizos, they were generally regarded as too poor to afford the alms necessary to secure the privileges of the Crusade Bulls. Hence, this motive influenced the exceptions to fast and abstinence dating back to Pope Paul III.

Nine years after the mitigations granted in 1852, Pope Pius IX granted a further indult on July 21, 1875, which reduced the fasting days for all ecclesiastic persons, except indios to consist of only eight days: Ash Wednesday, Holy Wednesday, Holy Saturday, Ember Friday in Whitsuntide, Ember Friday in September, Ember Friday in Advent, the Vigil of St. Joseph, and the Vigil of the Annunciation (if it did not occur during Pascaltide).

Dei Praesidio Suffulus details what transpired after this indult:

> This new request by Don Gregorio in 1865 was carefully worded: *quoad ieiunii legem, non*

vero quoad abstinentiæ (only the law of fasting, and not the law of abstinence). This means that while non-natives could enjoy the exemption from fasting granted to the indios, they could not, however, excuse themselves from abstaining on those previously held fast-days. If, however, they invoke the privileges of the Crusade Bulls, whereby they might consume flesh meat, they could not eat between meals.

On 2 May 1867, through a decree from the Sacred Congregation of Rites, Pius IX curtailed the number of precept days in Spain, an act which generated some confusion concerning whether the suppression also applied to overseas provinces (in Spanish, *provincias ultramarinas*), including the Philippines. Pius IX commanded that the exercise of fasting once observed in the vigils of feasts now suppressed, provided that by reason of Lent or Ember Week the fast was not anticipated, be transferred to the Fridays and Saturdays of Advent. On 9 May 1878, through a rescript from the same Congregation, Leo XIII extended the decree to all inhabitants of the Philippines, except to the canonical indios.

This rescript postdated the indult of 21 July 1875 by almost ten years. By virtue of its recentness (1878), it nullified the concession of the indult (1875), exacting observance only of the exercise that it (1878) prescribed. On 18 March 1885, Leo XIII granted a further indult upon the Philippine Islands, proroguing the indult for the exemption from fasting for another ten years.[116]

Hence by the end of the 1800s, the days of fasting and abstinence differed in the Philippines depending on whether one was an indio or not, as well as if someone were able to invoke the privilege of the Crusade Bulls. In practice, only a few days were obligatory days of fasting and abstinence for all (i.e., Fridays in Lent including Good Friday, Holy Saturday, and Christmas Eve). Other exceptions might apply as well such as when Ember Friday in Advent fell on the Feast of the Expectation of the Blessed Virgin Mary, as it did in 1892. Because of this feast, which was celebrated with the rank of Double Major in the Philippines, no one was bound to either fast or abstain that particular year on that day.

Further noting the decline of penance in these islands, *Dei Praesidio Suffulus* mentions that by reason of custom, dairy products and animal fat were also consumed on fasting days:

> Among the customs that the first period introduced, without any indult whatsoever, was the consumption of dairy products by the clergy, both regular and secular, and the use of animal fat in preparing the collations for fast days. The force of these came from neither universal nor particular law, but from the principle of *mos contra legem*, whereby a long-established custom always trumped or took precedence over the law.[117]

Consequently, the relaxation of fasting and abstinence was not only an American phenomenon. Devotion was fading throughout the world.

Armenian Fasting Traditions Retained in the Late 1800s

By the end of the 1800s, as fasting had already faded from its previous rigor, some groups which had long separated from union with the Roman Pontiff continued nevertheless to persist in the rigors of fasting. One such group was the Armenians.

Armenia is an ancient nation and the first nation to ever make Christianity the official state religion – back in 301 AD. By way of contrast, the Roman Empire made Christianity its official state religion in 380 AD. Modern day Armenia is bordered by Georgia to the north, Azerbaijan to the east, Iran to the south, and Turkey to the west. Its capital and largest city is Yerevan.

Today there are 350,000 Armenian Catholics located in Armenia, Syria, Iran, Iraq, Lebanon, Turkey, Egypt, Greece, Ukraine, Russia, France, Romania, United States, and Argentina. However, most Armenians are Orthodox, not in union with Rome. It is estimated that there are between 8 and 10 million such Armenian Orthodox Christians worldwide. The majority of Armenian Orthodox Christians live in Armenia, where the Armenian Apostolic Church is the national church. There are also significant Armenian Orthodox communities in countries such as Lebanon, Syria, Iran, Russia, and the United States.

St. Gregory the Illuminator is the patron saint and first official head of the Armenian Apostolic Church. He was responsible for converting Armenia from paganism to Christianity in 301 AD. However, the 'seeds' for Armenia's Christianity were planted by St. Bartholomew and St. Jude, two of the Twelve Apostles (also known as Nathaniel and Thaddeus, respectively). St. Bartholomew converted the king. The king's brother was enraged and, fearing a Roman attack, had St. Bartholomew flayed alive and beheaded. Tradition holds that while St. Jude helped evangelize the area, he was martyred in Syria. Some of his relics, however, were transferred to Armenia and preserved at the Saint Thaddeus Monastery which is located in present-day northern Iran.

Concerning the fasting observed by the Armenians by the end of the 1900s, Dr. James Issaverdens writes:

> In this point the Armenian discipline resembles that of the first ages of the Church; the utmost rigor is observed in all their fasts. They divide their fasts into three classes: Those are called Bahk, on which days they eat neither meat, eggs, milk-diet, nor fish, only vegetables, and their abstinence is so severe that they deprive themselves even of oil and wine.
>
> The second fast is called Dzuom and resembles the Bahk, with this difference, that only one meal a day is allowed to be taken after Vespers. The third fast is called Navagadik and allows the use of any food except meat. The Armenians are so faithful in the observance of these fasts that there is no dispensation from them and [they are] greatly scandalized on observing the slackness of European Christians who come in contact with them.
>
> Abstinence, during Lent, belongs to the first and second kind of fasting; this period begins on Monday, or two days before that of the Latins, and lasts until Easter Eve, when after the long service and the celebration of Mass, they break their fast with milk-diet only; but the Sundays in Lent make an exception to the general rule of abstinence as food may be taken at any hour.[118]

Dr. Issaverdens further notes that their strictness includes periods outside of Lent as well:

During the year they make frequent abstinences for many days, also for many weeks, such as one week before Septuagesima Sunday, in remembrance of the fast of Nineveh, and of the conversion of the Armenians to Christianity, commanded by St. Gregory the Illuminator. One week before Christmas and one about a month before also. A week before the feast of St. Gregory the Illuminator, the Assumption of the blessed Virgin, the Exaltation of the holy Cross, and before the Feast of the Transfiguration.

These are the principal fasts of the Armenians, but besides these we must mention the weekly fasting through the year which are every Wednesday and Friday, on which they abstain from meat, milk, butter, eggs, and oil; except in the week after the Nativity, Eastertide, and the Assumption.

The clergy, principally those dedicated to monastic life, live very austerely, and pass a good half of the year in rigorous abstinence.[119]

Fasting Changes in the Early 1900s

The *Catholic Encyclopedia* from 1909 in describing the law of fasting as it was immediately before the changes that occurred under St. Pius X, enumerates them as follows: "In the United States of America all the days of Lent; the Fridays of Advent (generally); the Ember Days; the vigils of Christmas and Pentecost, as well as those (14 Aug.) of the Assumption; (31 Oct.) of All Saints, are now fasting days. In Great Britain, Ireland, Australia, and Canada, the days just indicated, together with the Wednesdays of Advent and (28 June) the vigil of Saints Peter and Paul, are fasting days."[120]

While often held as an archetype for Tradition, the 1917 Code largely took the concessions granted to America and other nations and reduced fasting practices that were widely practiced elsewhere precisely at a time when our Blessed Mother appeared in Fatima, Portugal and called for an increase of penance and reparation.

The days of obligatory fasting as listed in the 1917 Code of Canon Law were the forty days of Lent (including Ash Wednesday, Good Friday, and Holy Saturday until noon); the Ember Days; and the Vigils of Pentecost, the Assumption of the Blessed Virgin Mary, All Saints, and Christmas. Partial abstinence, the eating of meat only at the principal meal, was obligatory on all weekdays of Lent (Monday through Thursday). And of course, complete abstinence was required on all Fridays, including Fridays of Lent, except when a holy day of obligation fell on a Friday outside of Lent. Previously, all Holy Days of Obligation, except for Christmas Day, required a special dispensation. Per the 1917 Code, Saturdays in Lent were likewise days of complete abstinence. Fasting and abstinence were not observed should a vigil fall on a Sunday as stated in the code: "If a vigil that is a fast day falls on a Sunday the fast is not to be anticipated on Saturday but is dropped altogether that year."

Why did Holy Saturday fasting only last until noon? The answer likely dates to when the Vigil Mass for Easter was moved from the night of Holy Saturday into Easter Sunday back to the morning of Holy Saturday. By the High medieval period, the celebration in the morning of the Easter Vigil (and other Triduum services) was almost the universal custom, in large part due to the fasting regulations requiring the fast to last until after Vespers. As a result, sometime after 692 AD, the fast on Holy Saturday was modified to end at noon. The Deharbe Catechism in the 1800s refers to the fast ending at Noon, so it does predate the 1917 Code.

Effective per the 1917 Code of Canon law, the Wednesdays and Fridays of Advent were no longer fast days for the Universal Church. Wednesdays of Advent had previously been abrogated as fast days in America in 1837. Now Fridays in Advent likewise ceased being required days of fast not only in America but universally. The Vigil of St. Peter and Paul also ceased as a fast day on the Universal Calendar, although it had already been abrogated in the United States.

Concerning abstinence, eggs and milk (i.e., lacticinia) became universally permitted. Canon 1250 stated: "The law of abstinence prohibits meat and soups made of meat but not of eggs, milks, and other condiments, even if taken from animals." And Canon 1251 stated: "It is not forbidden to mix meat and fish in the same meal; or to exchange the evening meal with lunch."

Commenting on this passage, Rev. Winfrid Herbst writes and explains more as it concerns lard and broth specifically:

> Canon 1250 of the Code of Canon Law states that soup or broth made of meat is forbidden on days of abstinence. The same Canon Law allows the seasoning of food with animal fats. In all animals we find layers of tissue or lumps of fat distinct from the flesh itself. Out of these lard and other animal fats are gained. The white flesh of animals, which is also called fat, is flesh just the same as the lean or muscular tissues. When meat is fried (especially if it contains layers of the white or fatty flesh, e.g., in bacon), grease flows from it, usually called drippings. Drippings, lard, and other animal fats may be used in frying potatoes and in cooking other foods on days of abstinence. But the eating of food on days of abstinence in

which flesh meat has been cooked [e.g., beans baked with pork] is not allowed, even if the particles not 'cooked up' have been removed...[121]

Hence even if lard was permitted in the preparation of food, meat broth was still forbidden. The same can be said for meat bouillon, which is a broth made by stewing meat in water.

Dispensations From Abstinence Were Previously Required Even for Holy Days of Obligation Outside of Lent

The 1917 Code also introduced the radical notion that a Holy Day of Obligation would *eo ipso* overrule the requirement of Friday abstinence for any Holy Days of Obligation outside of Lent. Previously the only day that would automatically abrogate the requirement of Friday abstinence was Christmas Day, which went back only to the 1200s.

It must be further noted that the removal of the obligation of penance on Holy Days of Obligation outside of Lent, effective with the 1917 Code, only applies to areas that observe the day of precept. It is not based on the Roman calendar, as affirmed by the Commission on the Code as related in a 1924 article published in the American Ecclesiastical Review.[122]

For instance, when January 6th, the Feast of the Epiphany, falls on a Friday, per the 1917 Code, it is still a mandatory day of abstinence in America and France and other places where it is not a Holy Day of Obligation. In contrast, Canada, Rome, and places that keep it as a Holy Day do not have to observe fasting and/or abstinence on that particular Friday. This, however, only applies to a Holy Day of Obligation outside of Lent. And this change only started with the 1917 Code - beforehand, it was still a day of abstinence on Fridays

100

regardless of whether it was a day of precept or not, unless a specific dispensation was issued by the Pope himself.

Liquids Permitted on Fasting Days

As previously mentioned, around the 14th century water and other liquids became widely permitted to all classes of people – not just monastics – outside the meal on fast days. This had been so widely known and taught that the 1917 Code did not even comment on the use of liquids on days of fast. In commenting on the Church's law, Father Jone notes that while liquids do not violate the fast, this adage concerns liquids understood in the proper sense and not quasi-food items like milk shakes. In a similar vein, juices made from puree or pureed food would violate the fast:

> ...liquids, including milk and fruit juices, are allowed. The usual amount of cream in coffee or tea is permitted. Milk is understood as ordinary or homogenized but does not include such combinations as malted milk or milk shakes. However, combinations based on skimmed milk and coloring or special flavoring such as chocolate milk are rather a drink than a food and, therefore, permissible.[123]

Father Prümmer states the same with some additional language worth noting:

> There is a common saying that drinks do not break the fast, but only those things are to be classified as liquids which normally aid the digestion of food: therefore, any drink which has a notable nutritive value cannot be regarded as pure liquid, such as milk, chocolate made with milk. But wine, beer, coffee, and tea are permissible.[124]

Antoine Villien in "A History of the Commandments of the Church" published in 1915 provides a history of the origin of the frustulum and the collation while noting that the distinction between simple liquids from others that would break the fast. This distinction stretches back to at least the Middle Ages:

> To allow the meal to be taken at noon was to render it possible to work harder in the afternoon but then the fatigued body required some refreshment at night. A little liquid to quench the thirst was at first permitted for it was held that liquids did not break the fast. The Church refrains from forbidding liquids because their primary function is to relieve thirst and aid digestion rather than to nourish although, as St Thomas admits, liquids do give some nourishment. However, the liquids in common use, water and wine, do not always suffice; they are not even an aid to digestion for everybody. Since there are other liquids more beneficial to digestion and better able to quench thirst, e.g., the *electuaria, viz.* more or less liquid jellies, preserves, candied fruit; could not these *electuaria* replace water and wine? St Thomas thought that it was just as lawful to take them as to take any other medicine provided only that they be not taken in large quantities or as a food. The permissible quantity was not specified, and it devolved upon custom to determine it. Quantity like custom naturally varied in different localities. In the monasteries where everything was better regulated this little lunch consisting of fruit, herbs, bread, water, or wine was taken in common, while the Collationes of Cassian were read; hence the name collation was given it and an effort was

made so to limit the repast that it might never be equivalent to a full meal. Thus, the essence of the fast was saved.

The collation was for the night. But in the morning also the weakened stomach felt the need of some relief. Since liquid did not break the fast it could not be forbidden. Neither did the *electuaria* break the fast as we have seen above, provided they were not taken in too great a quantity or *per modum cibi*; hence they were likewise permitted. Water, wine, coffee were simple liquids; hot chocolate without milk was placed in the class of the *electuaria*: all were tolerated. A little bread is sometimes necessary with wine or coffee *ne potus noceat*, so as not to inconvenience delicate stomachs; hence it likewise was permitted and thus originated the morsel of food commonly called frustulum. So, it was still true that only a single meal was taken.[125]

Fasting Changes Continue Immediately After the 1917 Code

But additional changes quickly ensued even after the promulgation of the Pio-Benedictine Code. Mara Morrow, writing on the fasting days around this time, states:

In 1917 Pope Benedict XV granted the faithful of countries in World War I the privilege of transferring Saturday Lenten abstinence to any other day of the week, excepting Friday and Ash Wednesday. In 1919 Cardinal Gibbons was granted his request of transferring Saturday Lenten abstinence to Wednesday for all bishops' dioceses in the U.S. This permission, as well as the workingmen's privilege, were frequently renewed, but, after 1931, this permission was only on the basis of personal requests from individual bishops.[126]

Further, in 1931 Cardinal Fumasoni Biondi, the Apostolic Delegate to the United States, addressed the following to the American Bishops: "The Sacred Congregation of the Council, in a letter dated 15 Oct 1931, informs me that, in view of the difficulties experienced by the faithful in observing the laws of fast and abstinence on civil holidays, His Holiness, Pius XI, in the audience of 5 Oct. 1931, granted to all the Ordinaries of the United States, ad quinquennium, the faculty to dispense their subjects from the laws in question whenever any of the civil holidays now observed occurs on a day of fast and abstinence, or of abstinence."[127]

Changes to the Dominican Third Rule

Those familiar with religious orders will be familiar with the concept of Third Orders. The first order typically refers to the main branch of a religious order. It consists of the male members (e.g., monks or friars) who live in religious communities and are often, but not always, ordained priests. The second order typically refers to a branch of the same religious order, but this branch is composed of women. Second order communities are often referred to as convents or monasteries, and the women who belong to the second order are commonly nuns. Additionally, some orders may have third orders, which are associations of lay people who live according to the spirituality and principles of the original order while remaining in the secular world. One such religious order with a Third Order is the Dominican Order. While the Third Order Rule did not bind under penalty of sin, members were nevertheless asked to observe the letter and spirit of the rule.

The original rule of the Dominican Third Order was promulgated by Munio de Zamora in 1285. The Rule of Munio, slightly amended, received papal approval in 1405. This Rule survived for centuries, serving the laity and being adopted for other branches of the Dominican Family. Regarding fasting and abstinence, the rule stated:

> From the first Sunday in Advent until Christmas, let the brethren and sisters fast every day, and likewise from Quinquagesima Sunday until Easter. They shall also fast every Friday throughout the year and shall observe all the fasts of the Church. Those who desire to fast oftener, or to perform any other austerities, may do so with the permission of their superior, and by the advice of a discreet confessor.[128]

The Second Rule, that of 1923, adapted to the 1917 Code of Canon Law, was approved in 1932. Among the updates, the Rule watered down the suggested days of fasting and abstinence as follows:

> Besides the fasts and abstinences instituted by the Church, Tertiaries, if not legitimately hindered, should fast on the vigils of the Most Holy Rosary, Our Holy Father Saint Dominic, and Saint Catherine of Siena. Moreover, adhering to the spirit of penance characteristic of the Order and of the ancient Rule, they should observe the Fridays of the whole year as fasts and exercise themselves in other works of penance with the advice, however, of the Director or a discreet confessor.[129]

Thus, even religious orders weakened their fasting and abstinence prescriptions.

Reductions in Fasting Intensify under Pope Pius XII

Pope Pius XII accelerated the changes to fasting and abstinence as Father Ruff relates: "In 1941 Pope Pius XII allowed bishops worldwide to dispense entirely from fast and abstinence except on Ash Wednesday and Good Friday, provided that there was abstinence from meat every Friday, and fast and abstinence on these two days and the vigil of the Assumption and Christmas. Eggs and milk products were permitted at breakfast and in the evening."[130]

On January 28, 1949, the United States bishops issued modified regulations on abstinence in America again after receiving a ruling from the Sacred Congregation of the Council. Partial abstinence replaced complete abstinence for Ember Wednesdays, Ember Saturdays, and the Vigil of Pentecost.

1949 also saw changes to fasting in Spain and her territories, including the Philippines, as a missal from that time notes:

> By virtue of the decree of the Sacred Congregation of the Council, given in the 28th day of January 1949, combined with the Privilege of the Bull of the Holy Crusade, the law of fast and abstinence is modified in the following manner:
>
> - Days of fast only: Ash Wednesday
> - Days of abstinence only: All Fridays of Lent
> - Days of fast with abstinence: Good Friday and the Vigils of the Immaculate Conception and the Nativity of Our Lord.

- Fast and abstinence: The Vigil of the Nativity is anticipated on Ember Saturday.

Note: It is supposed that all faithful enjoy the privilege of the Bull and the bishops make use of the faculty that was granted to them.

Latin America and the Philippine Islands

By virtue of the pontifical indult, it is only obligatory:

Days of abstinence only, without fast: the four vigils:

1. Vigil of Christmas
2. Vigil of Pentecost
3. Vigil of the Holy Apostles Peter and Paul
4. Vigil of the Assumption

Days of fast and abstinence: Ash Wednesday and all Fridays of Lent

Days of fast only without abstinence: all other Wednesdays of Lent, Holy Thursday, and Ember Friday during Advent.

Before 1951, Bishops in the United States were also able to dispense laborers and their family members from the laws of abstinence, if necessary, under the workingmen's privilege that was introduced in 1895. This privilege of eating meat excluded Fridays, Ash Wednesday, Holy Week, and the Vigil of Christmas. In 1951, the abstinence laws in America were again revised as Father Ruff summarizes:

In 1951 the U.S. bishops standardized regulations calling for complete abstinence from meat on Fridays, Ash Wednesday, the vigils of Assumption and Christmas, and Holy Saturday morning for everyone over age seven. On the vigils of Pentecost and All Saints, meat could be taken at just one meal. Fast days, applying to everyone between 21 and 59, were the weekdays of Lent, Ember days, and the vigils of Pentecost, Assumption, All Saints, and Christmas. On these fast days only one full meal was allowed, with two other meatless meals permitted which together did not make up one full meal. Eating between meals was not permitted, with milk and fruit juice permitted. Health or ability to work exempted one.[131]

As a result, the Vigil of All Saints was reduced to partial abstinence for American Catholics only in 1951. In 1954, Pope Pius XII issued a special decree granting bishops the permission to dispense from Friday abstinence for the Feast of St. Joseph which that year fell on a Friday.

The faithful alive in 1955 saw some of the most significant changes to the Church's Liturgy since the Council of Trent. Pope Pius XII in *"Cum nostra hac aetate"* on March 23, 1955, abolished fifteen Octaves in addition to the Octave for the Dedication of a Church, and octaves for patrons of various religious orders, countries, and dioceses. He also abolished roughly half of all vigils, leading to the removal of the liturgical vigils of the Immaculate Conception, Epiphany, All Saints, and All of the Apostles except Ss. Peter and Paul. The total number of liturgical vigils was now reduced to 7.

Uncertainty existed on whether fasting was still required on October 31st, the Vigil of All Saints (commonly called Halloween). The United States Bishops requested an official determination from Rome on whether the law of fasting and abstinence on the suspended Vigil of All Saints had also been terminated. They received a pre-printed notice in a response dated March 15, 1957, stating: "The Decree of the Sacred Congregation of Rites... looks simply to the liturgical part of the day and does not touch the obligation of fast and abstinence that are a penitential preparation for the following feast day." The US Bishop thereafter dispensed both the fast and partial abstinence law for the Vigil of All Saints.

In 1956, Holy Saturday was commuted from complete to partial abstinence. Furthermore, the fast which previously ended at noon was extended to the midnight between Holy Saturday and Easter Sunday, on account of the Holy Week changes enacted by Pius XII. In some places the previous ending at noon continued where custom or concession prevailed. And on July 25, 1957, Pope Pius XII commuted the anciently observed fast in the Universal Church from the Vigil of the Assumption to the Vigil of the Immaculate Conception on December 7, even though he had previously abrogated the Mass for the Vigil of the Immaculate Conception.

By the 1950s, the following guidelines concerning the law of abstinence were in force as explained by Father Dominic Prümmer:

> The law of abstinence forbids the eating of flesh meat and meal soup, but not of eggs, milk foods, and condiments made from animal fats. By flesh meat is meant a) the flesh of animals which live and breathe on land and possess warm blood; b) blood, lard, broth, suet, the marrow of bones, brains, kidneys. In case of doubt whether something is meat or not, one is permitted to eat it since the law does not bind when doubt exists.[132]

Fasting Changes Under John XXIII

On October 9, 1958, Pope Pius XII died. John XXIII was elected and under him, as under his predecessor, changes to Church discipline continued. In 1959, John XXIII permitted the Christmas Eve fast and abstinence to be transferred to the 23rd. While the United States, Great Britain, and Ireland kept the penance on December 24, other nations including Canada and the Philippines transferred it to December 23.

The Fasting Requirements of 1962

By 1962, the laws of fasting and abstinence were as follows as described in *Moral Theology* by Rev. Heribert Jone and adapted by Rev. Urban Adelman for the "laws and customs of the United States of America" copyright 1961:

> Complete abstinence is to be observed on all Fridays of the year, Ash Wednesday, the Vigils of Immaculate Conception, and Christmas. Partial abstinence is to be observed on Ember Wednesdays and Saturdays and on the Vigil of Pentecost. Days of fasting are all the weekdays of Lent, Ember Days, and the Vigil of Pentecost. If a vigil falls on a Sunday, the law of abstinence and fasting is dispensed that year and is not transferred to the preceding day.[133]

Father Jone adds additional guidance for the Vigil of the Nativity fast: "General custom allows one who is fasting to take a double portion of food at the collation on Christmas Eve (*jejunium gaudiosum*)."

Thus, even before the Second Vatican Council opened, both fasting and abstinence were drastically reduced within only a few hundred years. But even for the remnant that remained, the implications affected even secular business operations. For instance, Lou Groen, a Cincinnati-based McDonald's franchise owner, developed the Filet-O-Fish in 1962 after realizing that his business was hurting specifically on Fridays since the Catholic-heavy area of Cincinnati was not able to eat the chain's burgers on Fridays. And for a similar reason, public schools would by and large offer meatless options for children on Fridays. Restaurants with daily specials will still often have meatless specials for Fridays.

The Alleged Turkey Indult

A question often arises concerning an alleged indult granted to Americans to exempt them from abstinence on the Friday after Thanksgiving. The dispensation from meat on the day after Thanksgiving was granted in 1962 in the form of quinquennial faculties given to local ordinaries to dispense from abstinence on the Friday after Thanksgiving Day, as stated by Bouscaren in the *Canon Law Digest*. The quinquennial faculties lasted for five years only unless they were renewed. After this point, there was no need to because of *Paenitemini* and, more importantly, because of the November 1966 decree by the National Conference of Catholic Bishops (NCCB), which made abstinence on all Fridays throughout the year "especially recommended" but not obligatory. Thus, the privileges expired.

Before 1962, the Bishops in the United States did not generally dispense from Friday abstinence on the Friday after Thanksgiving. It may be argued that some bishops may have invoked the ability to dispense abstinence with the Friday after Thanksgiving as a holiday, which was made possible due to faculties granted to local ordinaries as early as 1931, but no concrete examples confirm this.

The only proof of these "turkey indults" comes from 1962 and after. In 1963 the Bishop of Little Rock, Arkansas made use of these privileges and dispensed the faithful from meat on the Friday after Thanksgiving:

> By reason of special faculties, His Excellency, the Most Reverend Bishop, grants herewith the following dispensations: from the Law of Fast on the Feast of St. Joseph, Tuesday, March 19; from the Law of Abstinence on Friday, November 29, (day after Thanksgiving) and from the Laws of Fast and Abstinence on Saturday, December 7, Vigil of the Feast of the Immaculate Conception.[134]

Such a dispensation from the law of abstinence was not permanently part of Church law by virtue of it being the Friday after Thanksgiving. The aforementioned privileges granted in 1962 have expired. Consequently, it is not appropriate to apply a "turkey indult" nowadays since there was no permanent indult to allow the use of flesh meat on the Friday after Thanksgiving in the United States.

The Lenten Observance
A Comparison of Regulations

Characteristics of Lent	Nicene 5th Century	Gregorian 7th Century	High Medieval 13th Century	Pre-Trent 15th Century	Benedict XIII 1724 - 1730	Benedict XIV 1740 - 1758	Baltimorensis II 1866	Leo XIII 1878 - 1903	Baltimorensis III 1884	CIC/17 1917	USA '62 1962
Collation & Frustulum											
Collation	No	No	Local Indults	Yes	Yes	Yes	Yes	Yes	Yes	Yes	Yes
Collation Size	N/A	N/A	Pint of Liquid	2oz	8oz/1/4 meal	8oz/1/4 meal	1/4 meal	1/4 meal	8oz	8oz/1/4 meal	8oz/1/4 meal
Morning Collation	N/A	N/A	No	No	No	No	No	No	Yes	Yes	Less than a 2nd meal
Animal Products at Collation	N/A	N/A	No	No	Yes	Local Indults	No	Local Indults	Yes	Yes	Yes
Warm Fish at Collation	N/A	N/A	N/A	N/A	N/A	Local Indults	No	Local Indults	Local Indults	Yes	Yes
Frustulum	N/A	N/A	N/A	No	No	No	No	Yes	Yes	Yes	Yes
Food											
Meal Time	Sundown	Sundown	3:00 PM	12:00 PM	12:00 PM	12:00 PM	12:00 PM	12:00 PM	12:00 PM	12:00 PM	N/A
Flesh Meat	No	No	No	No	No	Local Indults	No	Local Indults	Yes on some days	N/A	All but a few days
Fish & Flesh Meat at Meals	N/A	N/A	N/A	N/A	N/A	Local Indults	No	Local Indults	Yes, on some days	N/A	All but a few days
Animal Products	No	In necessarily only.	Yes	Yes	Yes	Local Indults	Yes	Local Indults	Yes	Yes	Yes
Simple Fish	No	No	Yes	Yes	Yes	Yes	Yes	Yes	Yes	Yes	Yes
Rich Seafood	Yes	No	No	No	No	No	Yes	Yes	Yes	Yes	Yes
Xerophagiae	Yes	Yes	No	No	No	No	No	No	No	No	No
Passion Fast	Yes	Yes	No	No	No	No	No	No	No	No	No
Sunday Abstinence	Yes	Yes	Yes	Yes	Yes	Yes	Yes	Yes	No	No	No
Beverages											
Liquids Other than Water and Wine	No	No	Local Indults	Yes	Yes	Local Indults	Yes, from meat	Yes	Yes	Yes	Yes
Wine	No	Yes	Yes	Yes	Yes	Yes	Yes	Yes	Yes	Yes	Yes
Water Outside of Meal	No	No	Yes	Yes	Yes	Yes	Yes	Yes	Yes	Yes	Yes

Fasting Changes Post Vatican II

Shortly after the close of the Second Vatican Council, Paul VI issued an apostolic constitution on fasting and abstaining on February 17, 1966, called *Paenitemini*, whose principles were later incorporated into the 1983 Code of Canon Law. *Paenitemini* allowed the commutation of the Friday abstinence to an act of penance at the discretion of the local ordinaries and gave authority to the episcopal conferences on how the universal rules would be applied in their region. Abstinence which previously began at age seven was modified to begin at age fourteen. Additionally, the obligation of fasting on the Ember Days and on the remaining Vigils was abolished. *Paenitemini* maintained the traditional practice that "abstinence is to be observed on every Friday which does not fall on a day of obligation."

The NCCB (precursor to the current USCCB bishops' conference of the United States) issued a statement on November 18, 1966. Abstinence was made obligatory on all Fridays of Lent, except Solemnities (i.e., First Class Feasts), on Ash Wednesday, and on Good Friday. Abstinence on all Fridays throughout the year was "especially recommended," and the faithful who did choose to eat meat were directed to perform an alternative penance on those Fridays outside of Lent, even though the US Bishops removed the long-establish precept of requiring Friday penance. The document stated in part: "Even though we hereby terminate the traditional law of abstinence binding under pain of sin, as the sole prescribed means of observing Friday, we... hope that the Catholic community will ordinarily continue to abstain from meat by free choice as formerly we did in obedience to church law." And finally, fasting on all weekdays of Lent was "strongly recommended" but not made obligatory under penalty of sin.

The 1983 Code of Canon Law largely took Paul VI's apostolic constitution aside from the modification of the age at which fasting binds. Per the 1983 Code of Canon Law, the age of fast was changed to begin at 18 – previously it was 21 – and to still conclude at midnight when an individual completes his 59th birthday. Fasting and complete abstinence per these rules were made obligatory only on Ash Wednesday and Good Friday. The notion of "partial abstinence," introduced under Pope Benedict XIV in 1741, was also removed along with nearly all fast days.[135] Friday penance is required per these laws on all Fridays of the year except on Solemnities, a dramatic change from the previous exception being only on Holy Days of Obligation.

Likewise, the USCCB's *Questions and Answers About Lenten Practices* also breaks with tradition by permitting broth and soup made from meat:

> Abstinence laws consider that meat comes only from animals such as chickens, cows, sheep, or pigs—all of which live on land. Birds are also considered meat. Abstinence does not include meat juices and liquid foods made from meat. Thus, such foods as chicken broth, consommé, soups cooked or flavored with meat, meat gravies or sauces, as well as seasonings or condiments made from animal fat are technically not forbidden. However, moral theologians have traditionally taught that we should abstain from all animal-derived products (except foods such as gelatin, butter, cheese, and eggs, which do not have any meat taste).[136]

Historical Evidence Confirms Even Holy Days of Obligation in Lent were not Dispensed Automatically from the Laws of Either Fast or Abstinence

As previously mentioned, Pope Pius XII issued a decree granting bishops the permission to dispense from Friday abstinence for the Feast of St. Joseph which that year fell on a Friday. A March 26, 1954, article in *The Guardian* elaborates:

> Bishops throughout the world have been granted the faculty to dispense their faithful from the law of abstinence on the Feast of St. Joseph, Friday, March 19. The power was granted in a decree issued by the Sacred Congregation of the Council, which said it acted at the special mandate of His Holiness Pope Pius XII. The decree published in *Observatory Romano* made no mention of a dispensation from the Lenten fast.

As such, St. Joseph's Day did not permit the faithful to eat meat on Fridays in Lent unless such a specific dispensation was offered, which was very rarely done. This was also at a time when there were many other fast days in the year outside of Lent. Likewise, to those who maintain the 1917 Code's requirement to also fast all forty weekdays of Lent – which was observed since the early Church – St. Joseph's Day remains a day of fast. Surely St. Joseph would want us to produce worthy fruits of penance during this holiest season as we prepare for the Pascal mystery. And surely the same can be said of our Lady, the Most Blessed Virgin Mary, whose Annunciation we celebrate each year on March 25th.

Unfortunately, the 1983 Code of Canon Law which aligns with the many modernist changes in the Church weakly states:

The penitential days and times in the universal Church are every Friday of the whole year and the season of Lent. Abstinence from meat, or from some other food as determined by the Episcopal Conference, is to be observed on all Fridays, unless a solemnity should fall on a Friday. Abstinence and fasting are to be observed on Ash Wednesday and Good Friday (Canons 1251 – 1252).

The notion that a solemnity that is not even a Holy Day of Obligation would trump Friday abstinence in Lent is absurd and a radical departure from all our traditions. Such a notion comes from 1983 and never beforehand. For instance, even Christmas would not automatically dispense Friday abstinence until the 1200s, as Dom Guéranger writes in the Liturgical Year originally published in 1886:

> To encourage her children in their Christmas joy, the Church has dispensed with the law of abstinence, if this Feast falls on a Friday. This dispensation was granted by Pope Honorius III, who ascended the Papal Throne in 1216. It is true that we find it mentioned by Pope St Nicholas I, in the ninth century; but the dispensation was not universal; for the Pontiff is replying to the consultations of the Bulgarians, to whom he concedes this indulgence, in order to encourage them to celebrate these Feasts with solemnity and joy: Christmas Day, St Stephen, St John the Evangelist, the Epiphany, the Assumption of our Lady, St John the Baptist, and SS Peter and Paul. When the dispensation for Christmas Day was extended to the whole Church, these other Feasts were not mentioned.[137]

Previously before the 1917 Code, a dispensation was required by the Holy Father even on Holy Days of Obligation that fell outside of Lent. Two examples indicating this are Pope Leo XIII's 1890 dispensation for Assumption Day[138] and a 1907 dispensation issued for Canada for All Saints Day.[139] All Saints Day was at that time a Holy Day of Obligation in Canada.

The Catholic Encyclopedia writing on St. Pius X's *Supremi disciplinæ* indicates that fasting was abolished *eo ipso* only starting in 1911 for all Holy Days of Obligation (which were at the same time reduced to only 8):

> The present Motu Proprio institutes another important change in legislation. As feasting and fasting are incompatible Pius X has abolished the obligation of fasting as well as that of abstinence for the Universal Church, should such obligation coincide with any of the eight feasts, as above.[140]

In practice, we know that the exception was Lent. Lenten abstinence and fasting always remained unless explicitly dispensed from even after the weakening changes in the 1917 Code.

Maronite Fasting Guidance

While fasting and abstinence after Vatican II were all but eliminated in the Roman Catholic Church, fasting and abstinence are still practiced – though not always under penalty of sin – by Eastern Rite Catholics. For instance, the following guidelines were issued in 2023 by the Maronite Patriarch, His Eminence and Beatitude Mar Bechara Boutros Cardinal Rai, for Maronite Catholics:

- Fasting from midnight to midday on all weekdays from Ash Monday to the Saturday of Light (8 April [this year]): no food or drink is to be consumed, with the exception of water.
- Abstaining from consuming meat and dairy on the Fridays of Lent; and throughout the first and last week of Lent (Holy Week).
- Fasting and Abstinence on Saturdays and Sundays are not an obligation, with the exception of the Saturday of Light (Easter Saturday), where fasting and abstinence are to be observed.
- In 2023, the following feast days fall within the Lenten Season: St John Maroun (2 March), The Forty Martyrs (9 March), St Joseph (19 March), St Rafqa (23 March), The Annunciation (25 March). We do not fast or abstain on these feast days.[141]

Even with these guidelines, food and water are permitted when needed to take medicine, for those sick or elderly, and for school children. The guidelines end with the note: "A person who cannot fast or abstain may choose another form of penance."

In comparison, the Maronite Synod of 1736 stipulated the following regulations that were kept at least until the 1920s:

> 1. Great Lent from Quinquagesima to Easter: Abstinence every day; fasting every day except on Sundays and Saturdays (with the exception of Holy Saturday)
>
> 2. Apostles Lent: Abstinence four days from 25th - 28th June

3. Assumption Lent: Abstinence eight days 7th - 14th August

4. Christmas Lent: Abstinence twelve days 13th - 24th December

5. Abstinence every Wednesday and Friday except: from Christmas to Epiphany, the Friday before Great Lent, from Easter to Pentecost, June 24th and 29th; August 6th and 15th

6 Forbidden foods: Like most oriental Christians, the Maronites kept the Mosaic ban on eating blood, suffocated animals and certain animals considered impure; and which Oriental Church Councils have many times renewed.[142]

In this context, fasting forbids the consumption of food or drink until midday. And for abstinence, eating any meat, oil, wine, and animal products (e.g., eggs, milk, and cheese) was forbidden. Hence, even the Maronites saw a reduction in their fasting by the 20th century.

The Ukrainian Catholic Church also encourages its members to keep these traditional fasting periods: Great Lent, the Apostles' Fast, the Nativity Fast, and the Dormition Fast. To these, they also add "the Eve of Theophany, the Exaltation of the Cross and the Beheading of John the Baptist"[143] as fasting days, with wine and oil allowed.

Year-Round Friday Abstinence is Required for Roman Catholics by the 1983 Code of Canon Law

The following is quoted from the 1983 Code of Canon Law:

Canon 1249: All Christ's faithful are obliged by divine law, each in his or her own way, to do penance. However, so that all may be joined together in a certain common practice of penance, days of penance are prescribed. On these days the faithful are in a special manner to devote themselves to prayer, to engage in works of piety and charity, and to deny themselves, by fulfilling their obligations more faithfully and especially by observing the fast and abstinence which the following canons prescribe.

Canon 1250: The days and times of penance for the universal Church are each Friday of the whole year and the season of Lent.

Canon 1251: Abstinence from meat, or from some other food as determined by the Episcopal Conference, is to be observed on all Fridays, unless a solemnity should fall on a Friday. Abstinence and fasting are to be observed on Ash Wednesday and Good Friday.

And thus, Roman Catholics are required without exception to abstain from meat on Fridays in Lent. Roman Catholics are also required to abstain from meat on all Fridays of the year unless the Bishops Conference of that area allows an alternative penance to be performed. Many faithful Catholics however choose just to honor the tradition of fish on Fridays year-round instead of substituting an alternative. This is in line with Catholic Tradition and the 1917 Code of Canon Law which did not allow an alternative penance. In 2011, The Catholic bishops of England and Wales called on all Catholics in their territories to return to mandatory Friday abstinence.

Also worth mentioning, a person cannot transfer abstinence from Friday to a different day like Thursday or Saturday. It must take place on the day in question (i.e., Friday).

Laws of Fast and Abstinence Bind Mortally

To ignore the law of Friday abstinence is a mortal sin and not merely a venial sin. This was made clear by both Pope Innocent III in the 13th century and Pope Alexander VII in the 17th century who both assert that to violate the law of abstinence on a required day is a mortal sin. The Catholic Encyclopedia explains this rationale:

> The Church enjoins the ways and means whereby her subjects must satisfy the obligation of doing penance inculcated by natural law. Many of the Fathers allude to the exercise of ecclesiastical authority in reference to the obligation of abstinence. The disciplinary canons of various councils bear witness to the actual exercise of authority in the same direction. Texts of theology and catechisms of Christian doctrine indicate that the obligation of abstaining forms an element in one of the Commandments of the Church. Satisfaction for sin is an item of primary importance in the moral order. Naturally enough, abstinence contributes no small share towards the realization of this end. As a consequence, the law of abstinence embodies a serious obligation whose transgression, objectively considered, ordinarily involves a mortal sin. The unanimous verdict of theologians, the constant practice of the faithful, and the mind of the Church place this point beyond cavil. They who would fain minimize the character of this obligation so as to relegate all transgressions, save such as originate in contempt, to the category of venial sin are anathematized by Alexander VII [Cf.

Prop. 23, ap. Bucceroni, Enchiridion Morale, 145 (Rome, 1905)].

In fine, the Trullan synod (can. 58, ap. Hefele, 'History of the Councils of the Church', V, 231, Edinburgh, 1896) inflicts deposition on clerics and excommunication on laymen who violate this law. Furthermore, theologians claim that a grievous sin is committed as often as flesh meat is consumed in any quantity on abstinence days (Sporer, Theologia Moralis super Decalogum, I, De observ. jejunii, # 2, assert. II), because the law is negative, and binds semper et pro semper.[144]

If you cannot resist having meat on Friday, how can you possibly resist more insidious assaults from the devil? The same can be said for a day of fasting – if you cannot refuse food for a short time, how can you reject serious temptations against purity, humility, or pride?

How & Why to Fast

Shared Days of Penance Matter

What is even more concerning than losing these traditions and connections with our forefathers is that the Church has taught that days of communal penance are more efficacious than mere private penances. The trend to encourage private fasting and penances and reduce Church-wide fasting to only Ash Wednesday and Good Friday is deplorable. Accordingly, Dom

Guéranger writes in his article on Ember Wednesday for September (contained in his 15-volume series on the Liturgical Year):

> We have already spoken of the necessity of private penance for the Christian who is at all desirous to make progress in the path of salvation. But in this, as in all spiritual exercises, a private work of devotion has neither the merit nor the efficacy of one that is done in company with the Church, and in communion with her public act; for the Church, as bride of Christ, communicates an exceptional worth and power to works of penance done, in her name, in the unity of the social body.[145]

He continues by quoting the following passage from Pope St. Leo the Great:

> God has sanctioned this privilege, that what is celebrated in virtue of a public law is more sacred than that which depends on a private regulation. The exercise of self-restraint which an individual Christian practices by his own will is for the advantage of that single member; but a fast undertaken by the Church at large includes everyone in the general purification. God's people never are so powerful as when the hearts of all the faithful join together in the unity of holy obedience, and when, in the Christian camp, one and the same preparation is made by all, and one and the same bulwark protects all...[146]

The Physical Benefits of Fasting

While the many spiritual benefits of fasting are clear from the Church's heritage – and as evident by the fact that all other major world religions encourage or also mandate fasting to a degree – there are also clear physical benefits for those who fast. On this point, the research published in *Nutrients*, a peer-reviewed, open access journal of human nutrition, states:

> Protocols of fasting roughly follow three modalities: whole-day fasts, time-restricted feeding, and alternate-day fasting, better known as intermittent fasting. Nowadays, intermittent fasting (IF) is the most popular and touted way to lose weight and increase lifespan. However, IF has other noticeable effects: in addition to reducing body weight, it affects glucose regulation, reduces systemic inflammation, and ameliorates some cardiometabolic parameters. IF can be difficult to integrate in a daily routine, chiefly because of the social norms and conventions about eating. On the other hand, fasting is the simplest form of dieting, convenient in terms of saving money and saving mental energy, usually used to think what to eat and when to eat.[147]

With the restriction of eating only once a day in the evening, the Church's fast days can be categorized as a form of intermittent fasting. And while we should pursue fasting chiefly for the honor of God and the good of our souls, God has blessed such intermittent fasts with physical benefits as well. As the journal further concludes based on research studies:

Recently, IF has been studied in several pilot studies, has been compared to calorie restriction and most importantly has been declared as a prevention factor for many diseases, regarding metabolic issues, heart disease, brain illnesses and cancer.[148]

Likewise, while fasting should not be undertaken for the primary purpose of losing weight, this added benefit would surely help the health of many as obesity rates climb in America and other developed nations:

In summary, from the available research it appears that IF programs are able to reduce body weight (3–7% on average), body fat (3–5.5 kg on average), total cholesterol (10–21%), and triglycerides (14–42%) in normal-weight, overweight, and obese humans.[149]

Studies have even shown a reduction in cancer risks for those engaging in fasting:

In fact, if fasting is applied correctly, that is, without malnutrition, it might have cancer-preventive effects in the presence of carcinogens: multiple cycles of periodic fasting showed the same efficacy as chemotherapy in the treatment of some cancers in mice. On the other hand, fasting has been suggested to have positive effects on cancer treatment. Intermittent fasting for 2–3 days appears to protect mice from a variety of chemotherapy drugs' untoward effects. The mechanism of this effect is called differential stress resistance and is responsible for protection of normal cells, but not cancer cells during short-term starvation.[150]

The Church has, in fact, prayed for the faithful to observe Her fasting days which are ordered for both "body and soul": e.g., the collect in the Traditional Latin Mass for the Saturday after Ash Wednesday implores God:

> O Lord, be mindful of our supplications, and grant that we may devoutly observe this solemn fast ordained for the healing of soul and body. Through our Lord...[151]

The Environmental Benefits of Fasting

The original nature of animals is seen in Genesis 1:29-30 where animals, as created by God, were companions of man before the Fall. As early as Genesis 3:21 we see the utilitarian use of animals begin. For instance, animal skin was used by God for clothing for men and women. Before the Fall, animals, both carnivorous and omnivorous, were in good relationship with man and were obedient to him. This relationship changed after the Fall, in which animals began to act violently towards man out of fear of him (cf. Genesis 9:2-3). Despite this, mankind was tasked with caring for Creation and still has this responsibility.

In addition to the myriad of physical and spiritual benefits of fasting, the practice of both fasting and abstinence has a positive contribution to the environment and God's creation. One of the positive side effects of having all Catholics return to robust abstinence would be a reduction of carbon emissions as a study by the University of Cambridge explains:

> In 2011, The Catholic bishops of England and Wales called on congregations to return to meat-free Fridays. Just a quarter of the 5 million Catholics in England and Wales changed their dietary habits – yet this still

saved over 55,000 tonnes of carbon a year, the researchers found. This is equivalent to 82,000 fewer return flights from London to New York over the course of a year.

Around the world, 1.3 billion people identify as Catholic. A papal decree would reinstate the obligation to follow meatless Fridays across the entire global church, saving millions of tonnes of greenhouse gases. National bishop conferences could also reintroduce the requirement. 'For instance, even if only the United States Catholic bishops were to follow suit, the benefits would likely be 20 times larger than in the UK,' the study's authors write.[152]

Pączkis, Pancakes, & Carnival on Shrove Tuesday

For those who plan to keep the true Lenten fast (i.e., fasting for all forty weekdays of Lent and abstaining from all meat and all animal products all forty days of Lent, and on all Sundays), Fat Tuesday represents one last day of merriment. Unfortunately, this day has grown into a debauched celebration for many who hardly fast at all during Lent. For this reason, while we can observe Fat Tuesday by enjoying food – including Polish pączkis which are customarily eaten on this day – we should ensure that our merriment never turns to gluttony. Some cultures – like the English – adopted the custom of eating pancakes on Fat Tuesday – earning it the nickname of "Pancake Tuesday." This custom, like the Polish one, was observed because for centuries the use of any lacticinia (i.e., animal byproducts like cheese, butter, milk, or eggs) was forbidden for the entirety of Lent. We should consider adopting a similar observance with our Lenten fast.

To be precise, in Poland itself, Catholics would eat "pączki" on Fat Thursday, not Fat Tuesday, when they traditionally eat herrings. It is today still a universal custom throughout Poland, although most people have no idea of this Pre-Lent period. The reason was that from Quinquagesima Sunday on, Poles could not eat lacticinia (e.g., dairy products) and on Friday and Saturday they also fasted. Thus, the Thursday between Sexagesima and Quinquagesima was the last day to eat "paczki" in Poland.

The practice of observing Carnival celebrations was based on the approaching Lenten fast. The word "carnival" comes from the Latin words "carnis" (meaning meat or flesh) and "vale" (the Latin word for farewell). Carnival then became the last farewell to meat since meat was never permitted at all during Lent until the liberalizing changes of Pope Benedict XIV in 1741. Lent was always a season of complete abstinence for centuries.

The name "Shrove Tuesday" also expresses the ancient practice of the faithful to go to Confession on the day before Ash Wednesday. Ælfric of Eynsham's "Ecclesiastical Institutes" from c. 1000 AD states:

> In the week immediately before Lent everyone shall go to his confessor and confess his deeds and the confessor shall so shrive him as he then may hear by his deeds what he is to do [in the way of penance].

Father Weiser similarly remarks, "In preparation for Lent the faithful in medieval times used to go to confession on Tuesday before Ash Wednesday. From this practice, that day became known as 'Shrove Tuesday' (the day on which people are shriven from sins)."

Make it a resolution to go to Confession on Shrove Tuesday or the weekend before. Since none of our penance done in the state of mortal sin earns merit for us, starting our Lenten penance in the state of sanctifying grace is of the utmost importance. Likewise, voluntarily adopting some days of fasting (e.g., Wednesdays and Fridays) with Lenten strictness will help make the transition to the true Lenten fast easier. This was voluntarily done in former times and is still done in the Byzantine Catholic Church as Father Weiser notes:

> In the Latin Church many priests and people, as well as the religious, fasted voluntarily during the latter part of pre-Lent, especially from Quinquagesima Sunday on. In the Byzantine Church this fasting was officially regulated from early times. They started abstaining from meat on Sexagesima, which is therefore called 'Meatless." With Quinquagesima the Eastern Church began (and still begins) the abstinence from butter, cheese, milk, and eggs. Thus, in eastern Europe that day is called 'Cheeseless Sunday.'[153]

Who Is Exempt from Fasting or Abstinence?

While we have lost so much of our heritage with the collapse of Catholic fasting and abstinence, especially in Lent, which is the very "badge of Christian honor," there are still some who try to excuse themselves from the minimal amount required. And there are others who, in their zeal to restore the older discipline, do too great an injury to themselves. It is, therefore, a good question to ask who is rightfully dispensed from the law of fasting and abstinence. Do manual workers have to fast? Do pregnant women have to fast or abstain? The question is worth considering in light of the Church's clear teaching in past times.

While the earliest catechisms ever made (i.e., the Catechism of the Council of Trent and the Catechism of St. Peter Canisius) do not mention fasting regulations, subsequent catechisms did. The Catechism of Perseverance published in 1849 notes the following are exempt from the law of fasting: the sick, those in "hard labor," and those in poverty. Likewise, this Catechism notes that the law of fasting binds starting at 21 years of age, so those under 21 were not bound to fast either.

Yet for those classes of people who were dispensed from the law, the Catechism adds: "When we doubt as to the obligation of fasting, we must consult our confessor or a pious and experienced physician. When we cannot fast, we must perform some other good works, watch more carefully over our senses, and support our labor and sufferings with more resignation."[154]

Hence, those who were dispensed were not free to go about their day as usual. They were to spend sufficient time on other good works: besides fasting, the other two chief good works are prayer and almsgiving. Hence, the poor were enjoined to pray to a much greater degree.

Father Keenan, in his 1846 catechism, notes that those exempted from the law of fasting include those under age 21, the weak, pregnant women, nursing women, those in "heavy and laborious employments," and "the poor who are never certain of sufficient and regular food." In an era before refrigeration, due to the uncertainty that those in poverty would have enough food to live from day to day, the Church dispensed them from the strictness of the law, which at that time was more stringent than is ours today. Note that in this catechism, as in the Catechism of Perseverance, there is no exception to the law of abstinence. There are only exemptions to the law of fasting. As importantly stated throughout this history, these are two distinct laws that become obligatory at two different ages in a person's life.

Hay's Catechism from 1781 contains the oldest mention of the age of fasting in an English-language catechism. Bishop Hays mentions those exempt from the law of fasting include those under age 21, the old who "are able to take only a little at a time but require it frequently," both pregnant and nursing women, those who are subjected to hard labor such as "husbandmen and tradesmen," those who are obliged to travel on foot.

Bishop Hay counsels for these classes of people: "But though these are exempted from the obligation of fasting, yet they are still obliged to observe the rules of abstinence unless some other particular reason require the contrary, as is often the case with people in sickness, where not only the quantity but also the quality of the food must be dispensed with, as their disease, according to the opinion of physicians, may require it."

He importantly concludes by reminding: "And when any such dispensation is given, it is sometimes enjoined, and always supposed, that they make up for this indulgence by other works of piety, such as more frequent prayer, and works of mercy towards their fellow creatures in distress." He then goes on in Question 41 to comment on how too many seek exemption from laws of abstinence on account of health where, to the contrary, abstinence would be good for their health. In an important context, abstinence laws in place in the late 1700s required abstinence much more often than nowadays, including even on Sundays in Lent, and mandated abstinence from eggs and dairy products (exceptions aside).

Based on these catechisms, both pregnant women and nursing women were exempt from the law of fasting but not the law of abstinence. Unfortunately, the United States Conference of Catholic Bishops stated the following in their Lenten regulation guides in recent years, showing that the editors have conflated the law of fasting and abstinence as too many people do: "Those that are excused from fast and abstinence outside the age limits include the physically or mentally ill including individuals suffering from chronic illnesses such as diabetes. Also excluded are pregnant or nursing women."

Unless a traditional Catholic priest and a competent physician - ideally one who understands the sacredness of Friday abstinence - advise her not to abstain, a pregnant woman should not excuse herself from the law of abstinence on Fridays. Such a practice is not part of the Church's tradition. The Church requires only one day a week to abstain from the flesh meat of mammals and birds. Meat is, after all, not medically necessary.

Therefore, the Church traditionally notes as exempt from fasting the following groups of people:

1. Pregnant Women
2. Nursing Women
3. Manual Laborers who would be physically unable to work given the strictness of fasting.
4. Those who are seriously ill - not those with minor allergy symptoms or basic colds but those with true medical conditions (e.g., cancer, diabetes, the flu, etc.). It should also be noted that the poor diet of many in countries like the United States often falsely causes people to feel that they are ill with a blood sugar issue when it really is just a poor diet. Those who believe they are exempt from the law of fasting due to legitimate sickness should speak with a component physician and a priest.
5. The elderly, which presently starts at age 60.
6. Those under the age of fasting, which traditionally began at 21 but is now 18 (though in the Middle Ages, it began at age 10)

Even if someone is exempt from the law of fasting, such an individual is bound to make up for the dispensation with fitting acts of piety and other good works (e.g., prayer and almsgiving). And to prevent scandalizing others, they should not eat in a place where others may see them. As to abstinence, there is no exemption from the law unless medically necessary. On this latter point we do well to consider carefully Dom Guéranger's wise counsel:

> But it will be asked: "Are there, then, no lawful dispensations?" We answer that there are; and that they are more needed now than in former ages, owing to the general weakness of our constitutions. Still, there is great danger of our deceiving ourselves. If we have strength to go through great fatigues when our own self-love is gratified by them, how is it we are too weak to observe abstinence? If a slight inconvenience deters us from doing this penance, how shall we ever make expiation for our sins? For expiation is essentially painful to nature. The opinion of our physician that fasting will weaken us, may be false, or it may be correct; but is not this mortification of the flesh the very object that the Church aims at, knowing that our soul will profit by the body being brought into subjection?

> But let us suppose the dispensation to be necessary: that our health would be impaired, and the duties of our state of life neglected, if we were to observe the law of Lent to the letter: do we, in such a case, endeavor, by other works of penance, to supply for those which our health does not allow us to observe? Are we grieved and humbled to find ourselves thus unable to join with the rest of the faithful children of the Church, in bearing the yoke of Lenten discipline? Do we ask of our Lord to grant us the grace, next year, of sharing in the

merits of our fellow Christians, and of observing those holy practices which give the soul an assurance of mercy and pardon? If we do, the dispensation will not be detrimental to our spiritual interests; and when the feast of Easter comes, inviting the faithful to partake in its grand joys, we may confidently take our place side by side with those who have fasted; for though our bodily weakness has not permitted us to keep pace with them exteriorly, our heart has been faithful to the spirit of Lent.[155]

With similar sentiments, St. Sophia Ukrainian Greek-Catholic Church in The Colony, Texas notes:

The Church has always exempted small children, the sick, the very old, and pregnant and nursing mothers from strict fasting. While people in these groups should not seriously restrict the amount that they eat, no harm will come from doing without some foods on two days out of the week — simply eat enough of the permitted foods. Exceptions to the fast based on medical necessity (as with diabetes) are always allowed.[156]

Recovering from Fasting

After having concluded the Lenten fast – as well as other extended fasts such as St. Martin's Lent – it is prudent to return to eating regular amounts of food slowly over time. During extended fast periods, the body undergoes a transformation so that after the fast has ended, one does not need to eat as much to feel satiety. An article published in 2015 in the Smithsonian Magazine explains why:

The latest science suggests that chronic food restriction can actually affect how much you need to eat to feel full—with caveats. An upcoming study of fasting mice, conducted by Farrugia and Tamas Ordog at the Mayo Clinic, shows that reducing food intake by 20 percent over four weeks results in a reduction of several important cellular stomach wall factors, reducing the amount of food the stomach can accommodate.

'When you analyze the stomach, you find that the number of nerves, the number of pacemaker cells [which produce coordinated muscle contraction during digestion] and smooth muscle are found in significantly lesser number,' says Farrugia. 'So, the stomach capacity to relax does actually shrink when there is dietary restriction.' These mice also show delayed gastric emptying, which measures the time it takes for food to move through the stomach and into the small intestine.[157]

From a practical perspective, eating two meals instead of three is a way to return to normal life. Also, ensuring that the meal is well balanced in terms of nutrients will also be of aid. It is important that after having disciplined our body and bringing it into subjection (cf. 1 Corinthians 9:27) that we ensure it is well taken care of for the next fast and so that we can undertake the duties based on our state in life. Proper care of the body and the soul are both important.

The Discipline of the Senses

While not truly part of fasting, the discipline of the senses (e.g., eyes, ears) should also generally accompany those seeking to perform penance and grow in virtue. While fasting is a powerful means to bridle temptations and raise the mind to contemplate heavenly things, conquering human tendencies to sin also requires the proper use of all the senses. To this end, incorporating the suggestions of Father Athanasius Iskander as quoted from "Practical Spirituality" would be a worthwhile endeavor. For the discipline of the eyes, he counsels:

> There are many verses in the Bible that exhort us to discipline our eyes: "The light of the body is the eye: if therefore thine eye be single, thy whole body shall be full of light. But if thine eye be evil, thy whole body shall be full of darkness" (Matt 6:22-23). "And if thy right eye offend thee, pluck it out, and cast it from thee: for it is profitable for thee that one of thy members should perish, and not that thy whole body should be cast into hell" (Matt 5:29) "Whosoever looketh on a woman to lust after her hath committed adultery with her already in his heart." (Matt 5:28)

> In the old times keeping the eye pure was not very difficult. The commandment "Do not look upon a woman in lust" was not difficult to follow, for women in those days were properly dressed and mostly covered up. Today however it is very difficult to keep the eye from encountering offenses. Not only has the dress code become so offensive, but there are so many ways that the Devil, the salesman of sin, can introduce impurity into the eyes.

> Magazines and books are now filled with pornography, and it seems that society is gradually increasing its tolerance and indeed its desire for more and more explicit porn.

You go shopping and while standing in line at the cashier, your eyes are bombarded with offensive pictures from every direction. Grocery stores now have candy free lanes, I wish they would introduce porn free lanes.

Department stores are not any better. The variety of intimate apparel that is on display and the way it is displayed make it very difficult for the eyes to remain in their sockets. Even if you are just walking in a mall, the windows of many shops are filled with displays of intimate ware. As if this is not enough, some stores would exhibit those items worn by manikins. Billboards on public roads and public transportation are now showing a lot of material that offends the eye (or delights it, depending on whether your eye is single or evil.)

TV offers us a more animated version of the same. There is hardly a movie without some kind of porn in it, even cartoons.
The Internet has now equaled or even surpassed TV in the amount and variety of sinful sights it offers, and they are only a mouse click away.

In trying to wean the eyes from the depraved scenes it became accustomed to, it is good to reflect on what the Bible tells us. The Book of Genesis tells us that when "the sons of God saw the daughters of men that they were fair; and they took them wives of all which they chose." Gen 6:2 The results were disastrous, for we are then told, in Gen 6: 7, "And the LORD said, I will destroy man whom I have created from the face of the earth." Looking and lusting after women led to the destruction of mankind.

The story of David should be a reminder to us of how dangerous it is for the eye to wander about without control. How carelessness about controlling the eyes has turned the author of the Psalms into an adulterer and a murderer.

One should struggle unto the blood against all of the above. It is very difficult, but absolutely necessary for our salvation. It is one thing to encounter these things while walking or shopping and another thing to seek them, by looking for them on TV or the internet, or even worse by renting pornographic videos or buying pornographic magazines. The punishment is much more for the latter than the former.

Watching violence is also another sin. There is hardly any movie now without violence. Even cartoons are filled with very violent scenes. Many sports are violent. There is hardly a hockey game without a delicious bit of banging and stumping. An even more dangerous is the – so called "sport" wrestling. I know a few kids who are addicted to watching wrestling.

Parents should watch over their children and make sure that they are seeing only appropriate things for their ages. There are ways and means for preventing your children from watching porn on TV and the internet. You should investigate and install these things before getting the internet or cable into your house.

Looking with lust at foods and pictures of food is also to be avoided, especially during fasting. Remember that this is what Eve did, "And when the woman saw that the tree was good for food, and that it was pleasant to the eyes, ... she took of the fruit thereof, and did eat." (Gen 3:6) The rest is history. Today we are bombarded by so many bigger than life pictures of hamburgers, ice cream, and even Kit Kats that make any mouth water.[158]

Thus, even if we observe the letter of the law of fasting, we must still strive to observe its spirit. St. Bede the Venerable, while exhorting the faithful to fast, likewise advises:

...we must realize that the worst temptations and trials, whether brought by evil spirits or by men, can all be overcome by praying and fasting. Moreover, these serve us as singular means for making atonement when God's just answer has been stirred up by our sins. Now fasting, in a wider sense, means more than restrictions on food. It means keeping all the allurements of the flesh at a distance; indeed, keeping one-self from every sinful passion. Likewise, prayer, in a wider sense, must consist of more than mere words beseeching God's mercy; it embraces everything we do with a dedicated spirit of faith in the service of the Creator.[159]

The Size of the "One Meal"

While the Church does not stipulate the size of the one meal on a fasting day, in keeping with the spirit of the law, it is appropriate that the meal would be approximately the same size as a regular meal on a non-fasting day. While eating a larger meal, even a buffet, would not violate the letter of the law, it would violate the all-important spirit of the law of fasting.

Father Dominic Prümmer in his *Handbook of Moral Theology* also provides guidance on the duration of the meal:

> According to modern discipline the hour when this one full meal is taken is left to the choice of the individual, and therefore, he is free to interchange the times of the evening collation and the full meal. However, this meal must have a moral continuity and not be unduly protracted, for if there is a notable interruption (e.g., an interruption of half an hour) it would develop into two distinct meals. Authors are sufficiently agreed that on fast days the meal cannot lawfully be extended beyond two hours.[160]

Join the Fellowship of St. Nicholas and Commit to Fasting

For able-bodied Catholics seeking to integrate into their lives fasting and abstinence with the mind of the Church, I recommend starting with year-round Friday abstinence, fasting and abstaining all of Lent, and fasting and abstaining on the Church's most important vigils. Over time, continue to add to this until you are observing all the fasts as our forefathers did.

To aid you in this, the Fellowship of St. Nicholas mentioned in the Appendix of this book provides three tiers. Start with Tier 1 or Tier 2, if you can. And over time aim to increase your penance until you are observing Tier 3, which incorporates all traditional – and even some optional – days of fasting and abstinence. While the tiers borrow from the principles and practices of Catholic Tradition, there are some adaptions.

In one instance, all tiers forbid desserts on fasting days in keeping with the spirit of penance and mortification. While having a vegan dessert would not, even in times past, break the fast, it would not be in conformity with the spirit of the law. And our hope is to observe both the letter of the former laws and their spirit for the good of souls and for the increase in virtue.

To those wishing to do more, incorporating a black fast and the Passion Fast, which are beyond the minimums of the Fellowship, could also be powerful means to render honor to God and to make restitution for sin during Lent.

In practice, the black fast (i.e., only one meal consumed after sunset, complete abstinence from all meat and animal products) is most appropriate for Lent since the Church mandates the strictest fasting at this time. While the time of the meal gradually moved up from after sunset to 3 PM in the High Middle Ages before advancing to Noon in the 15th century, those looking to observe a more austere Lent should strive to practice some Lenten days as days of black fast – especially Fridays and during Holy Week. Other fasts throughout the year like St. Martin's Lent, the Assumption Fast, and the Apostles' Fast need not be times of Black Fast. The extra austere nature of the Lenten fast makes one better understand the gravity of Lent.

Connected with the "Black Fast" are xerophagiae and the Passion Fast, both of which were practiced by obligation in Lent before the 7th century. We may wish to add these practices to our spiritual toolkit next Lent. Take this to prayer and discern if God is calling you to this greater sacrifice.

An additional suggestion is to strive to reduce even water consumption on Good Friday to an absolute minimum out of love for our Lord who cried out from the Cross: "I thirst." If

Christ our God can experience thirst, why should we – while striving to observe the strictest Black Fast on Good Friday – satiate ourselves with an increased amount of water? If our health permits it, we could strive to reduce our liquid consumption to the least amount possible and prayerfully contemplate the words of Christ: "If any man thirst, let him come to Me and drink. He that believeth in Me…within him shall flow rivers of living water" (John 7:37-38). If our forefathers could fast from even water on fasting days in the very Early Church, can we not fast from water too on Good Friday at least until sunset?

In a similar vein, a 1905 church bulletin from St. Mary's Church in Barrie, detailing the Lenten regulations for the Archdiocese of Toronto, counsels: "The Faithful are recommended during Lent to abstain from all intoxicating drinks in remembrance of the Sacred Thirst of Our Lord on the Cross."[161] We, too, could adopt that discipline for the honor and glory of God.

What We Have Lost

Today the number of fasting days in the Universal Church, including in the United States, is sadly only two: Ash Wednesday and Good Friday. Where has the rhythm and rhyme of the Catholic life gone? Some also rightfully ask if these reductions have contributed on a macro level to the rise of obesity and adverse health effects on society.

While no authority in the Church may change or alter any established dogmas of the Faith, the discipline of both Holy Days of Obligation and fast days may change. The days of obligation and the days of penance are matters of discipline, not matters of dogma. Lawful authorities in the Church do have the power to change these practices.

In the observance of the two precepts, namely attending Holy

Mass on prescribed days and fasting and abstaining on commanded days, we obey them because the Church has the power by Christ to command such things. We do not abstain from meat on Fridays for instance because the meat is unclean or evil. It is the act of disobedience which is evil. As Fr. Michael Müller remarks in his familiar *Explanation of Christian Doctrine* from 1874: "It is not the food, but the disobedience that defiles a man." To eat meat on a forbidden day unintentionally, for instance, is no sin. As the Scriptures affirm it is not what goes into one's mouth that defiles a man but that disobedience which comes from the soul (cf. Matthew 15:11).

Yet, even with such a distinction, the Church has historically been wise to change disciplines only very slowly and carefully. As Archbishop Fulton J. Sheen once remarked, "It is a long-established principle of the Church never to completely drop from her public worship any ceremony, object or prayer which once occupied a place in that worship." The same may be said for matters concerning either Holy Days of Obligation or fast days. What our forefathers held sacred should remain sacred to us in an effort to preserve our catholicity not only with ourselves but with our ancestors who see God now in Heaven.

Perhaps we need to ask ourselves and our own families what we can do, even if not mandated by Church law, to recover these former holy days of obligation and fasting days. Fasting and abstaining from meat and animal products on the forty days of Lent, the days of Advent, the Vigils of feasts, Ember Days, Rogation Days, and Saturdays year-round would be commendable. In a similar manner, observing the Apostles' Fast or the Assumption Fast, which are still kept in the Eastern Churches, would also be praiseworthy for a Roman Catholic.[162]

Father Lew, commenting on the post-conciliar changes to Ember Days, admonishes priests accordingly in words that can similarly apply to the other lost days of fasting:

> True, modern canon law is silent about the Ember Days. But tucked away in an obscure corner of the 1970 missal is a reference to 'the Four Times, in which the Church is accustomed to pray to our Lord for the various needs of men, especially for the fruits of the earth and human labors, and to give him public thanks' (*Normæ Universales de Anno Liturgico, 45*). The same words remain in the 3rd editio typica of this missal, published in 2002. However, the 'adaptation' of these days is left to Bishops' Conferences: they can decide how many are to be observed, and when, and with what prayers. A couple of 'fast days' are duly marked on each year's Ordo for the church in England and Wales, one in Lent and one in October, with the suggestion of celebrating a votive Mass of a suitable kind. Surely so ancient a tradition as the Ember Days must not be allowed to fade away.[163]

Rediscover A Love of Fasting

The Church has over time reduced the requirements required under penalty sin, but She still implores the faithful to do more than the mere minimum. But are we? St. Francis de Sales remarked, "If you're able to fast, you will do well to observe some days beyond what are ordered by the Church."

The Complete History of the Eucharistic Fast

St. Augustine observes that "...it is clear that when the disciples first received the body and blood of the Lord they had not been fasting" (*Epis. 54*). But early on, the Church adopted the practice, later enriched into law, of a fast from all food and water in preparation for Holy Communion. This fast is known as the Eucharistic Fast. While fasting is usually described in terms of refraining from eating a certain amount, eating once a day, and breaking the fast at only certain times, this is quite distinct from the Eucharistic Fast which has its own history.

The Early Church Practiced a Eucharistic Fast from All Food Whatsoever

The oldest record we have of the Eucharistic Fast as a midnight fast is from Tertullian (c. 160 – 220 AD), who in Book II, Chapter 5 of *Ad Uxorem* references a fast from all other food before receiving the Eucharist: "Will your husband not know what it is which you secretly eat before taking any food?" In the same era, St. Hippolytus (c. 170 – 235 AD), in the *Apostolic Tradition*, writes, "The faithful shall be careful to partake of the Eucharist before eating anything else" (ch 36).

St. Basil the Great (329 – 379 AD) similarly admonished the faithful who approached the Holy Eucharist to observe a period of fasting though he does not cite it as originating at midnight:

> The Lord receives the faster within the holy chancel. He receives not him that is full of excess, as profane and unholy. For if you come tomorrow smelling of wine, and that rancid, how shall I reckon your crapula for fasting? Do not think it is because you have not just poured in unmixed wine, but because you are not pure from wine.[164]

Shortly thereafter, the Synod of Hippo in 393 codified the Eucharistic Fast as a complete fast from all food: "The Sacrament of the Altar shall be received only by those who are fasting, except on Maundy Thursday (*cena Domini*)." It was likewise codified in Canon 41 at the Council of Carthage in 419 AD:

> That the Sacraments of the Altar are not to be celebrated except by those who are fasting, except on the one anniversary of the celebration

of the Lord's Supper; for if the commemoration of some of the dead, whether bishops or others, is to be made in the afternoon, let it be only with prayers, if those who officiate have already breakfasted.[165]

Centuries later, St. Thomas Aquinas references this decree noting that the exception for Holy Thursday had been abrogated by the time of St. Augustine:

> The wording of this decree is in accordance with the former custom observed by some of receiving the body of Christ on that day after breaking their fast, so as to represent the Lord's Supper. But this is now abrogated, because as Augustine says it is customary throughout the whole world for Christ's body to be received before breaking the fast.[166]

St. Augustine bears further witness to the universality of a complete and total fast before Holy Communion – in both East and West – in his letter 54 to Januarius from 400 AD:

> Must we therefore censure the universal Church because the Sacrament is everywhere partaken of by persons fasting? Nay, verily, for from that time it pleased the Holy Ghost to appoint, for the honor of so great a Sacrament, that the Body of the Lord should take the precedence of all other food entering the mouth of a Christian; and it is for this reason that the custom referred to is universally observed.[167]

The writings of St. Ambrose around the same time (cf. *De Elia et Jejunio* 10, 33, 34) corroborate this universal practice. Similarly, St. John Chrysostom alludes to the severity of this fast when, in defending himself against a charge that he gave Holy Communion to someone who was not fasting, writes:

> If I have done this, then let my name be erased from the list of bishops and no longer stand in the book of the orthodox faith; for certainly, if I have done this, Christ will cast me out of His kingdom.[168]

By the time of the Council of Trullo in 691 AD, the exception for breaking the fast on Holy Thursday was abolished as decreed in Canon 29:

> A canon of the Synod of Carthage says that the holy mysteries of the altar are not to be performed but by men who are fasting, except on one day in the year on which the Supper of the Lord is celebrated. At that time, on account perhaps of certain occasions in those places useful to the Church, even the holy Fathers themselves made use of this dispensation. But since nothing leads us to abandon exact observance, we decree that the Apostolic and Patristic tradition shall be followed; and define that it is not right to break the fast on the fifth feria of the last week of Lent, and thus to do dishonor to the whole of Lent.[169]

As previously stated, the Council of Trullo was never accepted as one of the Ecumenical Councils. Two canons of the council (e.g., Canons 13 and 55) condemned certain Roman practices but by 711 AD, Pope Constantine, in a compromise, accepted the canons in the East as valid but allowed differing practices in the Western Church to continue.

Between St. Augustine and St. Thomas it is said that Pope St. Nicholas I in c. 850 AD reviled the idea of faithful eating before the liturgy, as the *American Ecclesiastical Review* relates: "St. Nicholas I categorically laid it down that it was wrong and unheard of, for good Christians, not only in Lenten seasons but even on high festivals, to allow any food to pass their lips before the public Mass was ended."[170]

St. Thomas Aquinas in the Summa further appeals to the testimony of St. Augustine showing that while the Lord gave His Body and Blood to His disciples after a meal, it was appointed to the government of the Church under the Apostles to establish the law of fasting before Communion. And they did so:

> The fact that our Lord gave this sacrament after taking food is no reason why the brethren should assemble after dinner or supper in order to partake of it or receive it at mealtime, as did those whom the Apostle reproves and corrects. For our Savior, in order the more strongly to commend the depth of this mystery, wished to fix it closely in the hearts and memories of the disciples and on that account He gave no command for it to be received in that order, leaving this to the apostles, to whom He was about to entrust the government of the churches (*loc. cit.*, ad 1).[171]

The Eucharistic Fast in the Eastern Church

Before and after 1054, the East similarly continued to enjoin a fast before the reception of Holy Communion, which stretched back to before the time of St. Augustine. This is attested to in various decrees compiled in the Byzantine Nomocanons, which are a collection of both civil and canon law.[172] The Nomocanon of Photios from 883 AD included earlier councils and Fathers in addition to the 102 canons of the Council of Trullo, the 17 canons of the Council of Constantinople from

861, and three canons substituted by Photios for those of the Council of Constantinople from 869.

The Nomocanon of Photios supplemented *The Rudder*, a body of law for the Eastern Orthodox Churches, which was published in 1800 by Patriarch Neophytos VII, compiled by St. Nikodemos the Hagiorite. He named it after *"pedalion"* which means "rudder" to denote that just as a rudder guides the ship so too must the Church's canons be a guide for the life of a Christian. Just as a captain turns the rudder either to the left or to the right, so should the spiritual father use it accordingly with a given person. So, while the canons may be what they are, they are not to understood in a purely legalistic way, but rather as guidelines towards growing in God and cultivating the likeness of God which we were created with.

These canons are fully Catholic in everything that does not contradict Roman decrees and customs. Therefore, Latin and Greek Catholics alike can gain wisdom from the Fathers from the Rudder.

These Eastern canons assert that fasting – just like all other ascetic practices – must only be followed according to the strength and health of each person. For instance, the 69th Apostolic Canon forbids fasting with harsh punishments (i.e., laicization for clerics and excommunication for laity) for those who are sick or have serious health problems. St. Basil the Great noted in his canons for the monks under his care that fasts "can be either made harsher or be relaxed by the confessor/spiritual father according to the person."

The Rudder, which quotes the Council of Carthage as decreeing that priests must offer the Sacrifice while fasting, nevertheless adds as commentary on the previously mentioned remarks of St. John Chrysostom:

Note, however, that not only this Canon XLVIII of Carthage decrees that priests must officiate on an empty stomach [as we say in English, though in Greek the same idea is expressed differently by saying "fastingly"] but Canon LVI of the same Synod states that this is also confirmed by the Synod held in Nicaea. Nevertheless, if anyone is in danger of dying, he must commune even after having eaten, according to Canon IX of Nicepohrus. When St. Chrysostom was blamed for having administered the Communion to some persons after they had eaten, he wrote in a letter to Bishop Kyriakos: 'If it is true that I did this, may my name be stricken from the book of bishops. But if they say this to me once, and start quarreling, let them consider St. Paul, who baptized a whole household right after supper. Let them also consider Christ Himself, who gave the Communion to the Apostles right after supper.' Hence it is evidence that those who are about to commune has permission up to midnight to drink water, and thereafter they must not put anything in their mouth until they have communed.[173]

The whole concept of fasting falls within the concept of a Christian way of life. When St. Nikodemos and Agapios were compiling the Pedalion from all the canons, their main purpose for doing this was to provide Christians with a guideline for their lives in the late 18th century. When fasting is mentioned in the canons it evokes the implicit concept of preparation which ties in with the general concept of the interdependence of orthodoxy and orthopraxy. By fasting one is creating in the body what already exists in the soul (i.e., as the soul hungers for Christ and to come in communion with the Holy Trinity, so the Christian is imitating that hunger in the body by fasting and its desire for sustenance), but at the same time it also becomes a confession of faith by proclaiming that our true sustenance is God. This coincides with the ancient understanding of the connection between food and knowledge that we gain knowledge of something by partaking of it.

Hippocrates had famously said we are what we eat, but even from a modern viewpoint concept of nutrition, we are nourished by what we "commune" with. Such a mindset persists in practice among Eastern Christians to this day. In the Byzantine Tradition, the custom of fasting from midnight to the reception of Holy Communion remained until the mid-20th century.

The Middle Ages & the Eucharistic Fast

Throughout the Middle Ages, the Roman Catholic Church maintained the obligation of fasting from all food and water throughout the night until the reception of the Most Holy Eucharist. The fast as originating from midnight to the time of Holy Communion is attested to by St. Thomas Aquinas who in the Summa writes:

> That this sacrament ought to enter into the mouth of a Christian before any other food must not be understood absolutely of all time, otherwise he who had once eaten or drunk could never afterwards take this sacrament: but it must be understood of the same day; and although the beginning of the day varies according to different systems of reckoning (for some begin their day at noon, some at sunset, others at midnight, and others at sunrise), the Roman Church begins it at midnight. Consequently, if any person takes anything by way of food or drink after midnight, he may not receive this sacrament on

that day; but he can do so if the food was taken before midnight (*loc. cit.* ad 4).[174]

The Angelic Doctor continues by further affirming that neither water nor medicine – even in small quantities – may be intentionally consumed without violating the Eucharistic Fast:

> First, there is the natural fast, which implies privation of everything taken before-hand by way of food or drink: and such fast is required for this sacrament... And therefore it is never lawful to take this sacrament after taking water, or other food or drink, or even medicine, no matter how small the quantity be (*loc. cit.* ad 5).[175]

Hence, no liquids were permitted before the Eucharistic Fast, even though by this time liquids were permitted outside of the mealtime on penitential fasting days (e.g., vigils, Lent, ember days, etc.)

By the time of the Council of Constance (1414 – 1418 AD) the exception for Holy Thursday was no longer observed as affirmed at Session XIII on June 15, 1415:

> ...it is for this reason that this present Council... declares, decides, and defines, that, although Christ instituted that venerable sacrament after supper and administered it to His disciples under both species of bread and wine; yet, notwithstanding this, the laudable authority of the sacred canons and the approved custom of the Church have maintained and still maintain that a sacrament of this kind should not be consecrated after supper, nor be received by the faithful who are not fasting, except in

case of sickness or of another necessity granted or admitted by law or Church...[176]

Trent Affirms a Midnight Fast

The Catechism of the Council of Trent published under the order of Pope St. Pius V in 1566 further teaches a complete fast from all food and water: "We are to approach the Holy Table fasting, having neither eaten nor drunk anything at least from the preceding midnight until the moment of Communion."[177]

While we know that this was the universal rule, Tradition shows that over time various exceptions were gradually eliminated, as similarly seen in the Liturgy through organic development. Even at this time, the unintentional consumption of food or water before receiving the Sacrament was not sinful. And neither was receiving Holy Communion as Viaticum without having observed the strict Eucharistic Fast in force.

The 1917 Code of Canon Law

By the turn of the 20th century, the Eucharistic Fast as practiced under the reign of Pope St. Pius X remained one of complete abstinence from all "food or drink" as the Catholic Encyclopedia published in 1910 testifies to:

> That Holy Communion may be received not only validly, but also fruitfully, certain dispositions both of body and of soul are required. For the former, a person must be fasting from the previous midnight from everything in the nature of food or drink. The general exception to this rule is the Viaticum, and, within certain limits, communion of the sick. In addition to the fast it is recommended with a view to greater worthiness, to observe

bodily continence and exterior modesty in dress and appearance. The principal disposition of soul required is freedom from at least mortal sin and ecclesiastical censure. For those in a state of grievous sin confession is necessary. This is the proving oneself referred to by St. Paul (1 Corinthians 11:28).[178]

The traditional Eucharistic fast of abstinence from all food and water, with limited exceptions, was enshrined in the 1917 Pio-Benedictine Code in Canon 858. Such a fast applied to priests as well as anyone approaching Holy Communion:

> Those who have not kept the natural fast from midnight are not allowed to receive, except in danger of death, or in case it should become necessary to consume the Blessed Sacrament to safeguard it against irreverence.[179]

Father Dominic Prümmer in his *Handbook of Moral Theology* writes in commentary on this law:

> The Eucharistic fast, i.e., abstinence from all food and drink from midnight immediately preceding reception. This is a universal and most ancient custom which has been confirmed by many Councils in the Code of Canon Law, cc. 808 and 858. The law of fasting admits of no parvity of matter either in the quantity of food and drink taken or in time. Three conditions are required in order that what is taken have the character of food or drink:
>
> a) it must be digestible, and accordingly such things as small bones, human nails or human hair do not violate the fast;

b) it must be taken exteriorly, because what is taken interiorly is not eaten or drunk in the proper sense of the word. This is not a violation of the fast to swallow saliva or blood from the teeth or nasal cavities;

c) it must be taken by the action of eating or drinking. Therefore, the fast is not violated by anything received into the stomach a) mixed with saliva, such as a few drops of water swallowed while cleaning the teeth, b) through the action of breathing, v.g. when a man smokes or inhales tobacco smoke, c) through the injection of a nutritive substance.[180]

He adds how the fast should be calculated by noting concerning midnight:

Midnight may be computed in accordance with solar or legal time (whether this be regional or otherwise).[181]

And most importantly he notes six exceptions from the eucharistic fast:

1. In order to complete the sacrifice of the Mass (after the consecration of at least the bread or the wine);
2. In order to preserve the Blessed Sacrament from irreverence;
3. In order to avoid public scandal (when, for instance, ill-repute would be incurred if the priest did not celebrate Mass);
4. In order to receive Viaticum;
5. In order that Holy Communion may be given to the sick who have been confined to bed for a month without any certain hope of speedy recovery. These may receive Holy Communion twice a week though they have taken

medicine or liquid food (c. 858, § 2). The words "liquid food" include anything that is drunk even though it is nutritive food, such as raw eggs (but not cooked eggs);

6. In order that catechumens may receive Holy Communion after tasting salt during their Baptisms.[182]

Hence, while the law requiring abstinence from all food and drink from midnight was one of universal law, there were several exceptions permitted in 1917, though the most common of which was Viaticum. Even in the centuries before the time of Pope Pius XII, the Church mandated a strict fast before reception of the Holy Eucharist but did prudently permit various unique exceptions. Yet even beyond the letter of the law, the spirit of the law always shone. And this is seen by the counsel given in the 1946 book "Questions of Catholics Answers" by Father Windfrid Herbst on Holy Communion at Midnight Mass:

> There is no special universal law for the Christmas midnight Mass. If there were any good reason for it, one might take food or drink just before twelve o'clock and yet receive Communion during the Mass. No sin would thereby be committed. However, it is to be strongly recommended that those who receive Holy Communion during the midnight Mass be fasting from at least 8:00 PM out of reverence for the Blessed Sacrament. One should have enough spirit of sacrifice to offer the Eucharistic Savior this little tribute of respect.[183]

Why eight PM? Father Herbst explains:

> We say 8:00 PM because when permission was granted some years ago that a Mass beginning at midnight might be regularly said at a certain

famous European shrine, at which Mass the faithful might also receive Holy Communion, it was expressly prescribed that they be fasting from 8:00 o'clock on. We here see the mind of the Church, legislating in a particular instance; and we say that this is at least the earnest wish of the Church in all instances, unless otherwise specified.[184]

The Historic Changes to the Eucharistic Fast in the 20th Century

In 1953, before changing the immemorial Eucharistic Fast, Pope Pius XII referenced both the Synod of Hippo and St. Augustine as testimony of this ancient discipline when he wrote in *"Christus Dominus"*:

> From the very earliest time the custom was observed of administering the Eucharist to the faithful who were fasting. Toward the end of the fourth century fasting was prescribed by many Councils for those who were going to celebrate the Eucharistic Sacrifice. So it was that the Council of Hippo in the year 393 issued this decree: *'The Sacrament of the altar shall be offered only by those who are fasting.'* Shortly afterward, in the year 397, the Third Council of Carthage issued this same command, using the very same words. At the beginning of the fifth century this custom can be called quite common and immemorial. Hence St. Augustine affirms that the Holy Eucharist is always received by people who are fasting and likewise that this custom is observed throughout the entire world.

Doubtless this way of doing things was based upon very serious reasons, among which there can be mentioned first of all the one the Apostle of the Gentiles deplores when he is dealing with the brotherly love-feast of the Christians. Abstinence from food and drink is in accord with that supreme reverence we owe to the supreme majesty of Jesus Christ when we are going to receive Him hidden under the veils of the Eucharist. And moreover, when we receive His precious Body and Blood before we take any food, we show clearly that this is the first and loftiest nourishment by which our soul is fed and its holiness increased. Hence the same St. Augustine gives this warning: 'It has pleased the Holy Ghost that, to honor so great a Sacrament, the Lord's Body should enter the mouth of the Christian before other food.'

Not only does the Eucharistic fast pay due honor to our Divine Redeemer, it fosters piety also; and hence it can help to increase in us those most salutary fruits of holiness which Christ, the Source and Author of all good, wishes us who are enriched by His Grace to bring forth.[185]

Effective with the promulgation of *Christus Dominus*, Pope Pius XII declared: "In the future it shall be a general and common principle for all, both priests and faithful, that natural water does not break the Eucharistic fast." Four years later on March 25, 1957, Pope Pius XII issued *Sacram Communionem* which mitigated the midnight fast from all solid food and all alcoholic beverages to merely three hours before Holy Communion. Non-alcoholic beverages were subject to a one hour fast, though water was permitted as stated in *Christus Dominus*. Yet even with these unprecedented alterations to a discipline that stretched back to the subapostolic age, the Holy Father counseled the faithful, if possible, to keep the former fast:

> We strongly exhort priests and faithful who are able to do so to observe the old and venerable form of the Eucharistic fast before Mass and Holy Communion. All those who will make use of these concessions must compensate for the good received by becoming shining examples of a Christian life and principally with works of penance and charity.[186]

Yet far from returning to these practices, the faithful have forgotten them altogether and even monastic communities have adopted the minimums imposed by the subsequent changes enriched in the 1983 code. This code incorporated further changes made by Pope Paul VI on November 21, 1964, and January 29, 1973. Canon 919 of the 1983 Code provides as a minimum:

> §1 Whoever is to receive the blessed Eucharist is to abstain for at least one hour before holy communion from all food and drink, with the sole exception of water and medicine

> §2 A priest who, on the same day, celebrates the blessed Eucharist twice or three times may consume something before the second or third celebration, even though there is not an hour's interval.

> §3 The elderly and those who are suffering from some illness, as well as those who care for them, may receive the blessed Eucharist even if within the preceding hour they have consumed something.

Hence the changes to the Eucharistic Fast initiated under Pope Pius XII were accelerated, leaving the Church with a virtually non-existent fast. Such a reality stands in sharp contrast to the testimony of the Fathers, the decrees of the Synods of old, and the example of saints like St. Fructuosus who would not even drink water on the day of his martyrdom.

If the fast preceding the reception of the Sacrament of the Altar was based on divine law, then not even the Pope could dispense from it. But as seen in practice, this is not the case. Father Francisco Suárez (1548 – 1617), a Spanish Jesuit who was the leading figure of the School of Salamanca movement at this time and regarded as one of the greatest scholastics after St. Thomas Aquinas, adds: "One thing is certain: the precept concerning the receiving of the Eucharist before all food and drink is not imposed *jure divino*." *Jure Divino* (Latin for "by divine law") was distinct from the precepts instituted by the Church which could be changed. Yet, even if the Church *could* change such a fast, which unmistakably stretched back to the Early Church, *why* would she do so?

The Allowance and Prevalence of Evening Masses Cemented a Change to the Immemorial Eucharistic Fast

The time of day in which the Holy Sacrifice of the Mass may take place is governed by the Church's law. As codified in Canon 821 of the 1917 Code of Canon Law: "The beginning of the celebration of Mass shall not occur earlier than one hour before dawn or later than one hour after noon." This law was based on the practice of the Apostolic Fathers who generally celebrated the Sacrifice of the Mass in the morning. Tertullian, writing before his death c. 220 AD bears witness to the Mass taking place very early in the morning: "We take also, in congregations before daybreak, and from the hand of none but the presidents, the sacrament of the Eucharist, which the Lord both commanded to be eaten at mealtimes, and enjoined to be taken by all alike."[187] Such a practice persisted for centuries and eventually became Church Law. Even before the legislation issued by Pope St. Pius V in 1566, special exception was sought by the Carthusians who in 1363 received from Blessed Urban V permission to say Mass before daylight – though the permission was to be used sparingly "since our Lord Jesus Christ, the brightness of eternal light, is immolated in the mystery of the altar, it is not fitting that this should be done in the darkness of night."[188]

Father Shawn Tunink summarized this development in his dissertation on the topic of evening Masses:

> Looking back over the development regarding the day and time of Mass throughout history, the following can be summarized. The first Mass was celebrated in the evening hours on a Thursday. Very quickly thereafter the focus shifted to celebrating Mass in commemoration of the resurrection rather than connecting back to the historical time and day of the Last Supper. This consisted principally in the shift to the placing of the weekly assembly on Sunday. The time for Mass still seems to have varied from place to place and no written restrictions to the morning hours can be found until the time of Pius V in 1566. By 1917, although the law then allowed Mass to be celebrated on every day of the week, the time for Mass was entirely restricted to the morning. This was somewhat of a break with the more fluid history but seems to have been aimed primarily at maintaining a connection between the celebration of the Eucharist and the morning appearances of Jesus after the resurrection.[189]

Christmas midnight Mass was governed by an exception. Hence, while the time in which Mass may traditionally be said is specified in the 1917 Code of Canon Law as no earlier than one hour before dawn, Canon 821 §2 provided the specific exception for the time of midnight Mass: "On the night of Christmas, the conventual or parochial Mass alone can be started at midnight, but not otherwise without apostolic indult."

Amid the turmoil of the Second World War, further exceptions were instituted in nations affected by the War as Father Tunink adds:

> In 1941 German bishops were given permission for evening Masses on Sundays and weekdays 'as need dictated.' The previously mentioned indult given to Cardinal Suhard was applied to prisoners of war. Finally, American priests who were serving as military chaplains and other priests serving those in the military were given the special permission of celebrating Mass up to 7:30 pm on Sunday and weekdays without exception.[190]

And in the years after World War II, more prelates sought permission from the Holy See to continue offering Masses in the evening. Such changes were in part a reason for Pope Pius XII universally changing the Eucharistic Fast. Yet, it was not until the mid-1960s that, expanding upon this, various bishops began to seek permission for the faithful to satisfy their Sunday obligation of Mass attendance at a Mass celebrated on Saturday evening. Even after clarification was issued in 1964 that Sunday must still be kept as a day free of servile work, the practice of many Catholics no longer matched this reality when anticipated Masses offered on Saturday evenings became widely practiced.

This indult existed in the United States up until the 1983 Code of Canon Law, which states in Canon 931: "The celebration and distribution of the Eucharist can be done at any day and hour except those which the liturgical norms exclude." The 1983 Law also stated: "A person who assists at a Mass celebrated anywhere in a Catholic rite either on the feast day itself or in the evening of the preceding day satisfies the obligation of participating in the Mass." In practice, the prevalence of evening Masses – anticipatory or otherwise – which occurred nearly simultaneously with the change to the immemorial Eucharistic Fast imposes immense difficulties on the faithful who strive to observe the midnight Eucharistic Fast.

The goal of the reduced Eucharistic fast was to allow for the proliferation of evening Masses. It was the goal of Pius XII and several bishops to account for the new developments of the industrial age, in a time when people began to work different hours than in the past. While this was a reasonable goal in theory, it is another example of the acquiescence of the Papacy and of the bishops to the weakness of modern man.

Evening Masses were common from around 200 AD until around 1000 AD. It was the practice of the Early Church to have evening Masses every day in Lent and Advent except on Sundays, and the faithful fasted sometimes from sunset to sunset and sometimes from midnight to sunset, even without a single drop of water. They prayed earnestly and received our Blessed Lord in Holy Communion daily throughout Lent and Advent.

Tertullian is explicit about this along with the afternoon Masses that were common on Wednesdays, Fridays, Saturdays, and on vigils. And yet for 800 years the whole Church joyously fasted from everything for the whole day before receiving the Lord in Holy Communion.

The Importance of Thanksgiving After Holy Communion

It is not enough to simply receive the Sacrament of Holy Communion and return to our pews as if nothing has happened. We must constantly live with gratitude in our hearts, especially in the 15 minutes after receiving Communion when the Lord's Real Presence is still within our bodies.

Pope St. Pius X gives the reason behind the necessity of thanksgiving after having received Our Divine Savior: "Since the sacraments of the New Law ... produce a greater effect in proportion as the dispositions of the recipient are better, therefore, one should take care that Holy Communion be...followed by an appropriate thanksgiving, according to each one's strength, circumstances, and duties."[191]

Priests use a book called the *Roman Ritual,* which gives directions to priests and faithful alike concerning how to correctly receive the Sacraments. And it includes this important part on the Act of Thanksgiving After Holy Communion:

> Moreover, the communicants should be warned not to leave church right after receiving, nor to engage in idle conversation nor to violate custody of the eyes, and neither to begin at once the reading of prayers from a book nor to expectorate, lest the Sacred Species fall from the mouth. Rather, as befits devotion they should spend some time in mental prayer, thanking God for this singular favor and at the same time for the Savior's sacred Passion, in memory of which this mystery is celebrated and consummated.[192]

Thus, after Holy Communion, we need to speak with Our Lord personally and reflect on the depth of His love for us. Pope Pius XII in his encyclical on the Sacred Liturgy published in 1947 similarly said:

> Such personal colloquies are very necessary that we may all enjoy more fully the supernatural treasures that are contained in the Eucharist and, according to our means, share them with others, so that Christ Our Lord may exert the greatest possible influence on the souls of all.[193]

The Holy Father continued:

> When the Mass is over... the person who has received Holy Communion is not thereby freed from his duty of thanksgiving; rather it is most becoming that, when the Mass is finished, the person who has received the Eucharist should recollect himself, and in intimate union with the Divine Master hold loving and fruitful converse with Him. Hence, they have departed from the straight way of truth who, adhering to the letter rather than the sense, assert and teach that when the Mass has ended, no such thanksgiving should be added, not only because the Mass is itself a thanksgiving, but also because this pertains to a private and personal act of piety and not to the good of the community.[194]

Therefore, the necessity of making Acts of Thanksgiving is not just for us as individuals, but also for the good of the Church. And this allows us to perform our duties of charity towards our fellow men. While not required under pain of sin like the

Eucharistic Fast, this practice is one that the faithful should be regularly taught to practice.

In a similar vein, St. John Chrysostom (347 – 407 AD) counseled those who receive our Lord in Holy Communion to fast and devote time after receiving to works of charity rather than mundane affairs like indulging in large meals:

> Is it not so, that at such times, immediately after Communion, drunkenness succeeds and contempt of the poor? And having partaken of the Blood, when it were a time for you to fast and watch, you give yourself up to wine and reveling. And yet if you have by chance made your morning meal on anything good, you keep yourself lest by any other unsavory viand thou spoil the taste of the former: and now that you have been feasting on the Spirit you bring in a satanical luxury. Consider, when the Apostles partook of that holy Supper, what they did: did they not betake themselves to prayers and singing of hymns? To sacred vigils? To that long work of teaching, so full of all self-denial? For then He related and delivered to them those great and wonderful things, when Judas had gone out to call them who were about to crucify Him. Have you not heard how the three thousand also who partook of the Communion continued even in prayer and teaching, not in drunken feasts and reveling? But thou before you have partaken fastest, that in a certain way you may appear worthy of the Communion: but when you have partaken, and you ought to increase your temperance, you undo all. And yet surely it is not the same to fast before this and after it. Since although it is our duty to be temperate at both times, yet most particularly

after we have received the Bridegroom.
Before, that you may become worthy of
receiving: after, that you may not be found
unworthy of what you have received.

What then? Ought we to fast after receiving? I
say not this, neither do I use any compulsion.
This indeed were well: however, I do not
enforce this, but I exhort you not to feast to
excess. For if one never ought to live
luxuriously, and Paul showed this when he
said, she that gives herself to pleasure is dead
while she lives (cf. 1 Timothy 5:6); much more
will she then be dead. And if luxury be death to
a woman, much more to a man: and if this done
at another time is fatal, much more after the
communion of the Mysteries. And do you
having taken the bread of life, do an action of
death and not shudder? Do you not know how
great evils are brought in by luxury?[195]

The Frequent Reception of Holy Communion During Lent

At certain times of the year, the Faithful were especially
encouraged to receive the august Sacrament of the Altar and
one of those times was during the fast of Lent. Pope Nicholas
I in his Letter to the Bulgars from 866 AD counsels:

You ask whether you should communicate with
the body and blood of the Lord every day
during greater Lent. We humbly pray to
omnipotent God and exhort you all most
vehemently that you do so, but [you should not
do so] if your mind is disposed towards sin; if
your conscience, perhaps because it is
unrepentant or unreconciled [with God], does
not accuse the mind for its criminal sins; and if

one of you has not been reconciled with the brother with whom you are at odds because of your own vice. For we judge that, when someone is bitten by their conscience concerning one of these things, receiving communion weighs him down with a great accusation more than it offers him a remedy. Indeed, according to the Apostle: He eats and drinks his own judgment [I Cor. 11:29]. But regarding this and those who in fact enter the church but do not communicate when the offering is made, the sacred canons adequately speak. These canons should be administered by the bishop who is to be ordained for you by our mediocrity with God's support. He then should reveal them to the priests, who hold the keys of knowledge, and make no less known to you the canons regarding the matters which are necessary and not forbidden.

In the meantime, only during Lent, which Church custom calls the 'greater [fast],' should one communicate every day, observing a longer duration. For one should always spend time in prayer, come together at the sacrifices of the faithful, and recall constantly to mind those words of the prophet in which it is said: Your will is found on the day of your fast [Is. 58:3]. Indeed if, with the consent of the spouse, one perhaps spends time in prayer with a clean body at some other time as well, how much the more on this day — a day upon which we give the tithes of our flesh to God, we imitate the Lord Himself in abstinence, and we rightly cut from ourselves not only illicit things, but also from many things which are allowed — should we not also renounce every pleasure and apply ourselves to the chastity of our mind and body, in order that we may licitly spend time in prayer![196]

The Conventual Mass and the Natural Fast

The traditional rubrics for the celebration of the Holy Sacrifice of the Mass call for Holy Mass to be offered after the canonical hour of None on vigils and Ember days. Prior to the changes under Pope Pius XII, would everyone receiving Our Lord in Holy Communion – priests and all the ministers – observe the complete fast until then? And if so, how should religious orders seeking to restore Tradition implement the traditional Eucharistic Fast?

None refers to one of the hours of the Divine Office. At certain points throughout the day, all the Church prays the same liturgy to God, and we are all united in this wonderful prayer. The purpose of the Divine Office is to sanctify time and our day, making us constantly in prayer before the Father. The Church encourages all of her faithful to regularly pray the Hours, especially in common.[197]

The Divine Office is immensely helpful to a life of grace, and it is a great grace to be able to enter the prayer of the Church before God. The main hours to pray are Lauds, Vespers, and Compline which are generally prayed in the morning, evening, and night respectively. Prime, Terce, Sext, and None are the little hours taking place at approximately sunrise, 9 AM, Noon, and 3 PM respectively. Matins, the first hour, is often prayed very early in the morning or night and usually immediately precedes Lauds. The hours of the Divine Office are, with limited exceptions, obligatory for priests and consecrated religious like monks and nuns. Prime was unfortunately abolished in the post-Vatican II Breviary.

The Church's rubrics in place when the Eucharistic Fast was from midnight until the time of Holy Communion state that the

Mass must begin after None, but it does not follow that None must always be celebrated at a certain hour (e.g., 3 PM). In support of this view is Canon 821 of the 1917 Code of Canon Law which states that Mass may commence, "From one hour before dawn until one hour after midday." It therefore follows that the rubric could not be interpreted as mandating that the hour of None be celebrated at 3 PM and Mass afterwards, since Mass was not generally allowed at that hour.

While debated, it is affirmed by Rev. Heribert Jone that Regulars (i.e., religious who take vows) such as the Benedictines have the privilege of celebrating Mass two hours before dawn, two hours after midnight, and as late as 2 hours after midday, but may with a just cause celebrate Holy Mass as late as three hours after midday.[198]

Likewise, Father Quigley in his 1920 work, *The Divine Office A Study of the Roman Breviary* states: "In the recitation, the times fixed by the Church for each hour should be observed. But the non-recital at those fixed times is never a mortal sin and is rarely a venial sin, unless their postponement or anticipation is without cause."[199]

In the modern age from around the time of the Council of Trent until today the rubric regarding the conventual Mass on some penitential days is understood as one that is anticipated. The rationale for this practice is due to the abrogation of the obligation to postpone the meal until 3 PM – or at least 12 PM – on most vigils and ember days, if not by decree at least by contrary custom, except in the places that have kept it.

St. Robert Bellarmine attesting to this fact said, "The ancients offered the holy mysteries between the third hour and the ninth, because on fasting days the fast was not broken until the ninth hour. But ordinarily now the mysteries are celebrated between the first hour, that is, dawn, and midday."[200]

Wednesdays, Fridays, the vigils of the apostles, and other minor vigils along with the ember days outside of Lent were semi-jejunia or half-fast days in the first millennium, meaning that the fast day meal was not allowed until 3 PM. This was almost universally practiced in both the East and the West. The Pedallion, the Didache, Tertullian, and St. Basil attest to this. By the time of Pope Gregory VII at the turn of the first millennium, Wednesdays, Fridays, and Saturdays were reduced to abstinence days except in those places that kept the original discipline such as in the East on Wednesdays and Fridays and in places such as Ireland which kept the Wednesday and Friday fast and in England which kept the Friday fast.

By the time of St. Thomas Aquinas, most places did not keep the time for fast on the ember days due to the severe relaxation of fasting discipline and yet St. Thomas expresses a wide-ranging time for Mass: "But since our Lord's Passion was celebrated from the third to the ninth hour, therefore this sacrament is solemnly celebrated by the Church in that part of the day."[201] He expounds upon the principle more clearly when he writes:

> As already observed, Christ wished to give this sacrament last of all, in order that it might make a deeper impression on the hearts of the disciples; and therefore, it was after supper, at the close of day, that He consecrated this sacrament and gave it to His disciples. But we celebrate at the hour when our Lord suffered, i.e. either, as on feast-days, at the hour of Terce, when He was crucified by the tongues of the Jews (Mark 15:25) and when the Holy Ghost descended upon the disciples (Acts 2:15); or, as when no feast is kept, at the hour of Sext, when He was crucified at the hands of the soldiers (John 19:14), or, as on fasting days, at None,

when crying out with a loud voice He gave up
the ghost (Matthew 27:46-50).[202]

The rubric itself is an expression of an ancient practice that
goes back to the time of the Apostles, which was fully
developed liturgically by the onset of the patristic era. It was
understood that Wednesdays, Fridays, and some other
penitential days of the year (e.g., most vigils) were days of
fasting where the meal could not be taken until after 3 PM.
Tertullian mentions the conjoining of this discipline with the
liturgy. He says that Wednesdays and Fridays and most vigils
were called semi-jejunio and station-days, which were days of
half-fast, referring to the time of the meal days. These days
were also ones of devotion where the faithful were expected to
fast until None, hear Mass, and receive Communion. Holy
Communion at this point was not received until after None or
3 PM.

This was practiced in most places including Rome, and it was
also practiced by St. Basil in the East. It continued to be the
practice until around the turn of the first millennium when the
Wednesday, Friday, and Saturday fasts were reduced to simple
abstinence for the Roman Church by Pope Gregory VII, the
aforementioned exceptions withstanding.

As a result, should monks who seek to restore tradition keep
the Eucharistic Fast on vigils and ember days until 3 PM? Yes,
if they can. Should they celebrate the Traditional Roman Rite
of Mass at 3 PM on those days? Absolutely. This is the ancient
and longest standing practice of the Church which was
abrogated to acquiesce to the weakness of men.

Should monks also celebrate Holy Mass and fast until 3 PM
on all days of Advent as well from the day after St. Martin
until the day before Christmas Eve inclusively? Yes. Should
monks fast from everything until sunset on the major vigils
(i.e., Christmas, Pentecost, Assumption) and on every day in
Lent? Yes. Can Mass be said at that hour? Yes, but generally

only by way of a custom against the rubrics. In an era when so few keep the Traditions of the Faith and so few hear Daily Mass or pray the Divine Office, it is a comfort to know that some Religious Orders have adopted the traditional discipline of our forefathers to restore all things in Christ. Yet even lay Catholics can help restore these traditions.

Return to Tradition

The Eucharistic Fast is set by the Church so that those who are to receive Our Lord in Holy Communion are more consciously aware of this sublime encounter. While the specifics of the Eucharistic Fast have undergone considerable changes in the past century, the fast remains a matter of grave obligation. To intentionally violate the Eucharistic fast is a mortal sin as Father Jone notes: "Communion is forbidden under grave sin to one who has broken his fast by taking even a small amount of food or forbidden drink."[203]

Let us endeavor to observe in our own lives the strictness of the traditional discipline of all fasting – including the Eucharistic Fast – in a time when so few do penance and in keeping with the admonishment of Pope Pius XII who, even while altering the ancient fast, implored "[all] who are able to do so to observe the old and venerable form of the Eucharistic Fast before Mass and Holy Communion."[204]

Questions for Future Editions

All Saints Church in Warsaw by Marcin Zaleski from 1863

While this guide to fasting and abstinence has sought to compile in one text the forgotten and often unknown history – which priests are not even taught as part of their formation – some questions remain. The following questions, which are still unanswered after several years of research will, if solved, be incorporated into future editions of the book:

1. When did the Apostles' Fast fall out of practice in the West?
2. When did Wednesday officially cease being a universal day of fasting?
3. When were animal products first allowed to be consumed on Wednesdays and Fridays throughout the year? That is, when did Lenten abstinence begin to differ from other days of abstinence?
4. When was fish first allowed to be consumed on the weekly Wednesday and Friday fasts?
5. When was the latest time to begin one's meal – a delineation between the penitential fasts and the Eucharistic fast.
6. When did the Holy Saturday fast first end at Noon?

The Fellowship of St. Nicholas

The Fellowship of St. Nicholas is a lay sodality championed by *A Catholic Life* in partnership with *OnePeterFive* and *Sensus Fidelium.* It is committed to putting into practice concrete means to save one's soul and assist the souls of our brethren.

Under the patronage of St. Nicholas, this fellowship intends to serve as a means for Catholic Traditionalists to band together and **make communal penance in reparation** for the sins of the clergy, for the conversion of sinners, for the restoration of the Catholic Faith, and the triumph of Christendom in every country, home, and heart.

While St. Nicholas is well known for his charity and generosity, it is seldom mentioned how strictly he observed the laws of fast and abstinence from his infancy, as the traditional Roman Breviary remarks in the lessons at Matins:

> Nicolas was born in the famous city of Patara in Lycia. His parents obtained him from God by prayer, and the holiness of his life was marked even from the cradle. When he was at the breast, he never would suck more than once on Wednesdays and Fridays, and that always after sunset, though he sucked freely on other days. This custom of fasting he never broke during his whole life.[205]

Using the Church's venerable history of fasting and abstinence as our guide, we band together to hold each other accountable and to earn greater merits for souls. As St. Leo the Great affirmed:

> The exercise of self-restraint which an individual Christian practices by his own will is for the advantage of that single member; but a fast undertaken by the Church at large includes everyone in the general purification. God's people never are so powerful as when the hearts of all the faithful join in the unity of holy obedience, and when, in the Christian camp, one and the same preparation is made by all, and one and the same bulwark protects all...[206]

Rule of Traditional Catholic Fasting for the Fellowship

All members of this sodality agree to commit, at a minimum, to Tier 1, which is beyond the minimum required by Church law. Members may also privately commit to either Tier Two or Tier Three at their own or their spiritual director's discretion. This is open to Catholics of any Rite, although those in non-Roman Rites are still nevertheless canonically bound to observe all obligatory days of fasting and abstinence in their Rite, which may exceed the days in any given tier of this fellowship.

TIER 1

This Tier takes the 1917 Code of Canon Law as a minimum (with some minimal changes)

ABSTINENCE

- No flesh meat (i.e., meat from mammals or fowl) is to be consumed on any Friday in the year with no exceptions[207]
- No flesh meat is to be consumed throughout all of Lent from Ash Wednesday through Holy Saturday inclusive (including Sundays).
- No flesh meat is to be consumed on any Ember Day, the Vigil of Ss. Peter and Paul (June 28), Vigil of the Assumption (August 14), the Vigil of All Saints (October 31), the Vigil of the Immaculate Conception (December 7), the Vigil of Christmas (December 24), the Vigil of Pentecost, and January 22 (transferred to January 23 when the 22nd falls on a Sunday) for the National Day of Penance for Human Life.
- No sweets may be consumed for the duration of Lent (e.g., cake, cookies, pie, candies, gummies, chocolate/candy bars, pastries, cupcakes, chocolate muffins, pudding/custard, ice cream, Nutella, fudge, truffles, pralines, bonbons, mochi)

FASTING

181

- Fasting is defined as one meal only a day that may not be consumed earlier than noon but preferably is consumed after 3 PM or even after sunset. If necessary, an optional evening *collation* and an optional morning *frustulum* is allowed.[208]
- Fasting is to be observed for the entirety of Lent (except for Sundays), the Ember Days, the Vigil of Ss. Peter and Paul (June 28), Vigil of the Assumption (August 14), the Vigil of All Saints (October 31), the Vigil of the Immaculate Conception (December 7), the Vigil of Christmas (December 24), the Vigil of Pentecost, and January 22 (transferred to January 23 when the 22nd falls on a Sunday) for the National Day of Penance for Human Life.

TIER 2

ABSTINENCE

Everything as above in Tier 1 with the following additions:

- No flesh meat (i.e., meat from mammals or fowl) is to be consumed on any Saturday in the year unless that day is a First-Class Feast or a former Holy Day of Obligation
- Abstinence for all of Lent (including Sundays) includes abstaining from all seafood (e.g., fish, shellfish) eggs and all dairy products (e.g., milk, butter, cheese). Hence, Lent is a vegan fast – not a vegetarian one. When "abstinence" is mentioned for all other fasts, abstinence refers only to flesh meat, unless otherwise noted.
- Abstinence on the Minor and Major Rogation Days.
- No flesh meat is to be consumed during St. Martin's Lent from November 12 until Christmas Day – except for Sundays, the Feast of the Immaculate Conception

(unless it falls on a Friday), and Thanksgiving Day in the United States of America

FASTING

Everything as above in Tier 1 with the following additions:

- The entirety of St. Martin's Lent in Advent (except for Sundays) are days of abstinence from flesh meat.

In this tier, the fast and abstinence that is omitted in years when a day falls on a Sunday is transferred to the preceding Saturday (as it was done before the 1917 Code of Canon Law changed this practice).

TIER 3

ABSTINENCE

Everything as above in Tier 1 & 2 with the following additions:

- Abstinence for the Vigil of the Purification of our Lady (February 1), the Vigil of Corpus Christi, the Vigil of St. Lawrence (August 9), the Vigil of St. Bartholomew (August 23), the Vigil of Ss. Simon and Jude (October 27), and for the duration of the Apostles' Fast (except on Sundays) and the Assumption Fast (except on Sundays).

FASTING

Everything as above in Tier 1 & 2 with the following additions:

- Fasting for the duration of Apostles' Fast in June (except on Sundays) and the Assumption Fast in

August (except on Sundays) along with the Vigil of St. Lawrence (August 9), the Vigil of St. Bartholomew (August 23), the Vigil of Ss. Simon and Jude (October 27).

In this tier, like the one above, the fast and abstinence that is omitted in years a day falls on a Sunday is transferred to the preceding Saturday (as it was done before the 1917 Code of Canon Law changes).

EXTRAS

- While not part of the Fellowship Tier, it is certainly praiseworthy to observe the practice of St. Michael's Lent. This fasting period begins on the Assumption (August 15) and ends on the feast of St. Michael (September 29). It excludes Assumption Day itself and all Sundays, which are never days of fasting although they may be days of abstinence if one so chooses to keep them as such. Although devotion to St. Michael's Lent lacks the sort of history behind Lent or the Assumption Fast and the like, the standard of 1 meal, 1 frustulum, and 1 collation would be a good rule to follow in observing it
- For the Eucharistic Fast, keep the 3 hours fast at a minimum, while striving to return to the midnight fast.

HOW TO JOIN

Any member of the lay faithful can freely commit to Tier 1, the base requirement for the fellowship. This commitment is a voluntary penance and failure to fulfill this commitment does not bind under pain even of venial sin. To participate, simply join the Telegram group here on desktop or mobile: https://t.me/+aXEK-WgNzL42NmJh.

Go to https://www.onepeterfive.com/fast for these rules and an annual fasting calendar published every year.

TESTIMONIALS OF THOSE IN THE FELLOWSHIP

The following testimonials come from those who joined the Fellowship of St. Nicholas in the first half of 2023.

"Bottom line is my entire self is so much better following what I did for Lent than anything previously. I don't know how else to explain; following the old way of fasting is awesome and I will continue. Completely understand now 'The Love of Fasting'" (Eileen S).

"He has Risen!! Alleluia Alleluia…Thank you Matthew and all members of this group. I felt so called and blessed to purchase Matthew's book and join this sodality. During this lent…for the first time I gave true penance to the Lord. I successfully adhered to Tier 2 and would like to continue throughout the year in Tier 3. The lights I received during these past 46 days are illuminating a path forward in establishing a Rule of Life. There is a new awareness and rhythm in blending liturgical, spiritual, and temporal areas together, creating a truly integrated Catholic life. I'm praying this is just the beginning of a life of complete surrender to the Lord…all for His glory. God Bless each and every person on this most important mission of communal reparation" (Christine C).

"I learned of Mr. Plese's important book through the *OnePeterFive* website, bought it, and joined the sodality. The experience was life-changing, to say the least. To be perfectly open, I'm over 60 and have never fasted this hard in my life. Nor did I do 100% of the requirements for Tier 1. The results were amazing, nonetheless. I found that giving up meat, except, in my case, for Sundays and major feasts, strengthened my will and sharpened my spiritual intuitions. Advances in the interior life were real: my prayer deepened, and I was given concrete, specific direction to follow, the following of which opened new vistas of insight and of action. Improvements in physical health were also real: acid reflux disease disappeared and sleep was deeper and more refreshing. The deeper sleep led to greater alertness in times of prayer and in sensitivity to others and their needs.

"The sodality was life-giving. People supported each other, people came clean when we failed, people got up and kept on going. Personalities began to emerge as we became a real band of brothers and sisters in the Lord. Advice flowed freely as people shared what did and did not work for them.

"As for permanent gains, the way I eat has changed: there is no going back to the habits that were serving me poorly, and I have greater resolution to address the challenges, spiritual and physical, that lie before me. I have a very special request to the Lord, which discretion impedes me from naming. He has given me the path for fulfillment of that request, and fasting is a major part of it. My experience here ties to the experiences of many — saints, blessed, and others on the way — who have found fasting to be a major component of the spiritual life. That is why I can say that if you decide to follow the path that Mr. Plese lays out for you, be prepared to be amazed" (David C).

Suscipe, Sancta Trinitas.

Endnotes

1 St. Basil, *Sermo de jejunio*, p. 31, 163, 98

2 St. Thomas Aquinas, Summa Theologiae II-II, Q. 147, a. 1, Accessed via https://www.newadvent.org/summa/3147.htm.

3 Accessed via https://acatholiclife.blogspot.com/2020/03/in-state-of-mortal-sin-we-gain-no.html.

4 Adalbert de Vogue, "To Love Fasting: The Monastic Experience," Translated by Jean Baptist Hasbrouck, (Saint Bede's Publications, 1989), Accessed via https://archive.org/stream/tolovefasting/To%20Love%20Fasting_djvu.txt

5 Rev. F.B. Jamison, "Catechism of Perseverance," Translated from the French of Monsignor Gaume, (James Duffy, 1866), p. 129.

6 https://archive.org/details/familiarexplana00mlgoog

7 Rev. Hugo Hoever, "Lives of the Saints," (Catholic Book Publishing Co, 1961), p. 144.

8 St. Francis de Sales, *Introduction to the Devout Life*, Chapter 23.

9 Epistola 25 ad Decentium 4; Patrologia Latina 20:555

10 Douay Catechism Accessed via https://archive.org/details/The1649DouayCatechismTubervilleHenryD.D.4515/page/n55/mode/2up.

11 Dom Guéranger, *The Liturgical Year: Lent* (Burns & Oates, 1912), p. 1.

12 Catechism of the Liturgy by a Religious of the Sacred Heart, (The Paulist Press, 1919), Accessed via http://catholicsaints.mobi/ebooks/book-articles/catechism-of-the-liturgy-for-young-and-old.htm.

13 *The Catechism of the Council of Trent* on the Sacrament of Baptism.

14 Francis X. Weiser, *Handbook of Christian Feasts and Customs* (New York: Harcourt, 1958), p. 187.

15 Karl Adam Heinrich Kellner, "Heortology: A History of the Christian Festivals from their Origin to the Present Day," (Kegan Paul, Trench, Trubner & Co, 1908), p. 99.

16 Rev. Stephen Keenan, *A Doctrinal Catechism*, p. 179, Accessed via, http://www.catholicapologetics.info/apologetics/protestantism/catechism.htm

17 Dom Guéranger, *The Liturgical Year: Lent* (Burns & Oates, 1912), p. 5.

18 Father Alban Butler, *The Moveable Feasts, Fasts, and Other Annual Observances of the Catholic Church* (James Duffy, 1839), p. 146.

19 Ibid.

[20] See http://holyunia.blogspot.com/2010/08/traditional-byzantine-rite-fast-and.html for a delineation.

[21] Father Alban Butler, op cit, p. 155.

[22] Johann Evangelist Zollner, "The Pulpit Orator Containing, for Each Sunday of the Year, Seven Elaborate Skeleton Sermons," Volume 2, (Pustet & Company, 1884), p 248.

[23] A Hymn in Honor of the Most Blessed Martyrs Fructuosus…, Peristephanon, Aurelius Prudentius, hymn 6, c.392.

[24] Tertullian, De Jejunio, X.

[25] Gabriel Meier, "St. Fructuosus of Tarragona." The Catholic Encyclopedia. Vol. 6. (Robert Appleton Company, 1909), Accessed via http://www.newadvent.org/cathen/06311b.htm.

[26] The Poems of Prudentius, translated by Sr. M. Clement Eagan, p. 168.

[27] Writing on Holy Thursday, Gregory DiPippo notes: "The earliest Roman sacramentaries attest to the custom by which the blessing of oil was done at a separate Mass from that of the Lord's Supper [on Holy Thursday], while a third Mass was celebrated for the reconciliation of the public penitents. The earliest form of this Mass given in the Old Gelasian Sacramentary makes it very clear why this was so." Accessed via https://www.newliturgicalmovement.org/2022/04/the-oldest-text-of-chrism-mass.html

[28] Catechism of the Liturgy, Accessed via http://www.pathsoflove.com/catechism-of-liturgy/chapter4/

[29] Ibid.

[30] "Sacramentarium Ecclesiæ Catholicæ. A Sacramentary designed to incorporate the contents of all the Sacramentaries anywhere used in the Church, previous to the sixteenth century. Part I. Advent and Christmas. Lat. & Eng" (Joseph Masters, 1857), p. ii.

[31] Fr. R. Janin, A.A. Les Eglises orientales et Les Rites orientaux, Paris, 1922

[32] Frederick Holweck, "Eve of a Feast." The Catholic Encyclopedia. Vol. 5. (Robert Appleton Company, 1909). Accessed via http://www.newadvent.org/cathen/05647a.htm

[33] Henry Robert Percival, The Seven Ecumenical Councils of the Undivided Church (Parker, 1900), p 391.

[34] St. Augustine, Epistle 36 to Casulanus, Accessed via https://www.newadvent.org/fathers/1102036.htm.

[35] Ibid.

[36] Translated by James Donaldson. From Ante-Nicene Fathers, Vol. 7. Edited by Alexander Roberts, James Donaldson, and A. Cleveland Coxe. (Christian Literature Publishing Co., 1886.). Revised and edited for New

Advent by Kevin Knight. Accessed via
http://www.newadvent.org/fathers/07152.htm.

[37] Henry Robert Percival, *The Seven Ecumenical Councils of the Undivided Church* (Parker, 1900), p 391.

[38] Jevsevije Popovic, Opca Crkvena Istorija (Sremski Karlovci: Srpska Manastirska Stamparija, 1912), p. 781.

[39] Francis Dvornik, *The Photian Schism*, (University Press, 1948), p. 130.

[40] St. Augustine, Epistle 36, to Casulanus

[41] Rev. Dominic M. Prümmer, *Handbook of Moral Theology* (The Mercier Press, Limited, 1949), p. 54.

[42] Dom Guéranger, *The Liturgical Year: Septuagesima* (Burns & Oates, 1909), p. 4.

[43] Francis X. Weiser, *Handbook of Christian Feasts and Customs* (New York: Harcourt, 1958), p. 155.

[44] Francis X. Weiser, *Handbook of Christian Feasts and Customs* (New York: Harcourt, 1958), p. 171.

[45] Father Alban Butler, *The Moveable Feasts, Fasts, and Other Annual Observances of the Catholic Church* (James Duffy, 1839), p. 1152.

[46] Ibid., p. 170.

[47] Laetare Sunday would eventually become the one day of a reprieve during the Lenten observance when at least in some places abstinence was relaxed.

[48] Francis X. Weiser, *Handbook of Christian Feasts and Customs* (New York: Harcourt, 1958), p. 171 – 172.

[49] Pope John XXIII, *Paenitentiam Agere*, (July 1, 1962).

[50] James A. Brundage. "Law, Sex, and Christian Society in Medieval Europe," (University of Chicago Press, 2009), p. 158.

[51] https://ruvid.org/ri-world/the-catholic-precept-of-not-having-sex-during-lent-was-maintained-until-the-end-of-the-franco-regime/

[52] Accessed via
http://www.stsophiaukrainian.cc/resources/thefastingseasons/

[53] J. D. O'Neill, "The Black Fast". *The Catholic Encyclopedia.* (Robert Appleton Company, 1907). Accessed via:
http://www.newadvent.org/cathen/02590c.htm

[54] Ibid.

[55] Rev. Leonard Goffine, "The Church's Year," Accessed via
http://www.sspxasia.com/Documents/The_Church_Year/

[56] Dom Guéranger, *The Liturgical Year: Pascal Time: Volume 2* (Burns & Oates, 1910), p. 395.

[57] Dom Guéranger, *The Liturgical Year: Pascal Time: Volume 2* (Burns & Oates, 1910), p. 133.

[58] Francis X. Weiser, *Handbook of Christian Feasts and Customs* (New York: Harcourt, 1958), p. 42.
[59] The Catholic Directory, Ecclesiastical Register, and Almanac (Burns and Lambert, 1861), p. 22.
[60] 1962 Roman Catholic Daily Missal, (Angelus Press, 2004).
[61] Francis Mershman, "Ember Days." *The Catholic Encyclopedia. Vol. 5.* (Robert Appleton Company, 1909). Accessed via http://www.newadvent.org/cathen/05399b.htm
[62] Ibid.
[63] Dom Guéranger, *The Liturgical Year: Advent* (Burns & Oates, 1910), p. 218.
[64] Father Alban Butler, *op cit.,* p. 149.
[65] Barefoot Abbey, "Everything You Need to Know about the Ember Days," Accessed via https://barefootabbey.com/2019/03/11/everything-you-need-to-know-about-the-ember-days/.
[66] Sacramentarium Ecclesiæ Catholicæ. A Sacramentary designed to incorporate the contents of all the Sacramentaries anywhere used in the Church, previous to the sixteenth century. Part I. Advent and Christmas. Lat. & Eng" (Joseph Masters, 1857), p. iii.
[67] Ibid.
[68] Dom Guéranger, *The Liturgical Year: Advent* (Burns & Oates, 1910), p. 24.
[69] Father Antonine Villien, "History of the Commandments of the Church," (B. Herder, 1915), p. 273.
[70] Monsignor Gaume, "Catechism of Perseverance," (Gill & Son, 1884), p 245.
[71] Father Antonine Villien, "History of the Commandments of the Church," (B. Herder, 1915), p. 276.
[72] Helen McLoughlin, *Christmas to Candlemas in a Catholic Home*, (The Liturgical Press, 1955).
[73] Ildefonso Cardinal Schuster, *The Sacramentary*, (Burns, Oates & Washbourne, 1924), p. 386.
[74] "The Little Flowers" & the Life of St. Francis with the "Mirror of Perfection" (Dutton, 1912), p. 383.
[75] "The Little Flowers of the Glorious Messer St. Francis and of His Friars," Translated into English by W. Heywood, (Methuen & Co, 1906), p. 146.
[76] Accessed via http://www.liturgialatina.org/raccolta/sacrament.htm.
[77] Joseph A. Gribbin, "The Premonstratensian order in late medieval England," (Boydell Press, 2001), p. 79.

[78] Accessed via https://deipraesidiosuffultus.wordpress.com/2014/03/03/fasting-and-abstinence-in-the-philippines-i/.

[79] Father Thomas Slater, "Cases of Conscience for English-speaking Countries," (Benzinger, 1911), p. 92.

[80] Accessed via https://www.elespanol.com/cultura/20190419/meco-pueblo-espana-no-pecado-viernes-santo/391961535_0.html

[81] Father Thomas Slater, "Cases of Conscience for English-speaking Countries," (Benzinger, 1911), p. 93.

[82] *The American Catholic Quarterly Review, Volume 11* (Hardy & Mahony, 1886), p. 465.

[83] Ibid.

[84] *The American Catholic Quarterly Review, Volume 11* (Hardy & Mahony, 1886), p. 466.

[85] Accessed via https://deipraesidiosuffultus.wordpress.com/2014/03/19/fasting-and-abstinence-in-the-philippines-ii/.

[86] Johan F. M. Swinnen and Mara P. Squicciarini, "The Economics of Chocolate," (OUP Oxford, 2015), p. 274.

[87] Translated by Joseph Berg, "A Synopsis of the Moral Theology of Peter Dens," (J.B. Lippincott & Co, 1856), p. 333.

[88] James MacCaffrey, "History of the Catholic Church from the Renaissance to the French Revolution," Volume 1, (M.H. Gill and Sons, 1915), p. 114.

[89] Don S. Armentrout and Robert Boak Slocum, "An Episcopal Dictionary of the Church, A User-Friendly Reference for Episcopalians." Accessed via https://www.episcopalchurch.org/glossary/days-of-abstinence/

[90] *The Irish Ecclesiastical Record* (1868), Volume 8, p. 221.

[91] Rev. Thomas Slater, SJ, "A Short History of Moral Theology," (Benzinger Brothers, 1909), p. 24.

[92] The Rule of St. Benedict in English, Translated by Timothy Fry, (Liturgical Press, 2016), p. 63.

[93] Rev. Paschasius Heriz, "Saint John Of The Cross," (College of Our Lady of Mount Carmel, 1919), p. 38.

[94] Simi & Segreti, St. Francis of Paola, Rockford, IL: Tan Books, 1977, p. 26.

[95] Ibid.

[96] George Ryan, "The Lenten 'Beer Only Fast' Practiced by German Monks," Accessed via https://ucatholic.com/blog/the-lenten-beer-only-fast-practiced-by-german-monks/

[97] Ibid.

[98] Dom Guéranger, *The Liturgical Year: Pascal Time: Volume 3* (Burns & Oates, 1909), p. 133.

[99] The Life of St. Charles Borromeo by John Peter Giussano provides in depth accounts of his heroic life and the example of penance he reached, even in the midst of a devastating plague. It may be read at https://archive.org/details/lifestcharlesbo01giusgoog/page/n8/mode/2up.

[100] Dom Guéranger, *The Liturgical Year: Advent* (Burns & Oates, 1910), p. 24.

[101] Father Antonine Villien, "History of the Commandments of the Church," (B. Herder, 1915), p. 305.

[102] Arthur Devine, "Convent Life, Or, The Duties of Sisters Dedicated in Religion to the Service of God," (R. Washbourne, 1897), p. 245.

[103] John Elihu Hall, Joseph Dennie, "The Port Folio," (Editor and Asbury Dickens, 1821), p. 141.

[104] "The Canadian Journal of Industry, Science and Art," (Canadian Institute, 1859), p. 387

[105] Sydney Watt, "Enlightened Fasting," Food and Faith in Christian Culture, Edited by Ken Albala and Trudy Eden, (Colombia University Press: 2011), p. 106.

[106] Accessed via https://www.detroitcatholic.com/news/the-history-of-detroit-catholics-muskrat-eating-tradition-and-yes-its-still-a-thing

[107] Maria C. Morrow, "Sin in the Sixties," (Catholic University of America Press, 2016), p. 121.

[108] Monsignor Gaume, "Catechism of Perseverance," (Gill & Son, 1884), p. 237.

[109] Accessed via https://archive.org/details/laitysdirectoryt00unse/page/n8/mode/1up.

[110] "The Jurist," Volume 12, (Catholic University of America School of Canon Law, 1952), p. 188.

[111] Maria C. Morrow, "Sin in the Sixties," (Catholic University of America Press, 2016), p. 122.

[112] "A Manual of Prayers for the Use of the Catholic Laity: Prepared and Published by Order of the Third Plenary Council of Baltimore," (Catholic Publication Society Company, 1888), p. 18.

[113] The 1905 Parish Guide of St. Mary's Church in Barrie accessed via https://archive.org/details/parishguidestmar00slsnuoft.

[114] Maria C. Morrow, "Sin in the Sixties," (Catholic University of America Press, 2016), p. 122.

[115] *The Handbook to Christian and Ecclesiastical Rome published* in 1897.

[116] Accessed via
https://deipraesidiosuffultus.wordpress.com/2014/04/04/fasting-and-abstinence-in-the-philippines-iii/

[117] Ibid.

[118] James Issaverdens, "The Sacred Rites and Ceremonies of the Armenian Church," (Armenian Monastery of St. Lazaro, 1876), p. 503 – 504.

[119] James Issaverdens, *op cit.,* p. 504

[120] J.D. O'Neill, "Fast." The Catholic Encyclopedia. (Robert Appleton Company, 1909). Accessed via https://www.newadvent.org/cathen/05789c.htm

[121] Winfrid Herbst, "Questions of Catholics answered," (Society of the Divine Savior, 1946), p. 235.

[122] Rev. Herman Joseph Heuser, *American Ecclesiastical Review* (Catholic University of America Press, 1924), vol. 71, p. 637 - 638.

[123] Rev. Herbert Jone, *Moral Theology* (The Newman Press, 1961), p. 263.

[124] Rev. Dominic M. Prümmer, Handbook of Moral Theology (The Mercier Press, Limited, 1949), p. 225 – 226.

[125] Father Antonine Villien, "History of the Commandments of the Church," (B. Herder, 1915), p. 265 - 266.

[126] Maria C. Morrow, "Sin in the Sixties," (Catholic University of America Press, 2016), p. 122.

[127] *Homiletic and Pastoral Review*, 32-416; E.R., 86-65, 190

[128] Accessed via https://motherofmercychapter.com/Rule.html

[129] Ibid.

[130] Rev. Anthony Ruff, OSB, "Fasting and Abstinence: The Story," Accessed via https://praytellblog.com/index.php/2018/02/21/fasting-and-abstinence-the-story/

[131] Ibid.

[132] Rev. Dominic M. Prümmer, *Handbook of Moral Theology* (The Mercier Press, Limited, 1949), p. 226.

[133] Rev. Herbert Jone, *Moral Theology* (The Newman Press, 1961), p. 261 – 262.

[134] Decree printed in *The Arkansas Catholic* (March 1, 1963), Accessed via http://arc.stparchive.com/Archive/ARC/ARC03011963p09.php.

[135] For a chart comparing 1917 v. 1955 v. 1983 fasting, please see Catholic Candle at https://catholiccandle.neocities.org/faith/fast-abstinence-basics.html.

[136] Accessed via http://www.usccb.org/prayer-and-worship/liturgical-year/lent/questions-and-answers-about-lent.cfm

[137] Dom Guéranger, *The Liturgical Year: Christmas: Volume I* (Burns & Oates, 1904), p. 127.

[138] Accessed via https://www.newspapers.com/article/the-times-leader/70691123/

[139] Accessed via https://www.newspapers.com/article/the-ottawa-citizen/70692138/.

[140] Andrew Meehan, "Supremi disciplinæ" *The Catholic Encyclopedia.* (Robert Appleton Company, 1912). Accessed via: https://www.newadvent.org/cathen/14342a.htm

[141] Accessed via https://www.maronite.org.au/auto-generate-from-title-2/258-lenten-penitential-practices,-2023.html.

[142] Fr. R. Janin, A.A. Les Eglises orientales et Les Rites orientaux, Paris, 1922

[143] Accessed via http://www.stsophiaukrainian.cc/resources/thefastingseasons/

[144] J.D. O'Neill, "Abstinence." The Catholic Encyclopedia. Vol. 1. (Robert Appleton Company, 1907). Accessed via http://www.newadvent.org/cathen/01067a.htm

[145] Dom Guéranger, *The Liturgical Year: Time After Pentecost: Volume II* (Burns & Oates, 1909), p. 388.

[146] Dom Guéranger, *op cit.*, p. 390.

[147] Visioli, F.; MucignatCaretta, C.; Anile, F.; Panaite, S.-A. Traditional and Medical Applications of Fasting. Nutrients 2022, 14, 433, Accessed via https://doi.org/10.3390/ nu14030433.

[148] Ibid.

[149] Ibid.

[150] Ibid.

[151] 8th Edition of the Monastic Diurnal published by St. Michael's Abbey Press.

[152] Charlotte Elton, "Meat free Fridays: Catholic tradition could slash global carbon emissions, study finds," Accessed via https://www.euronews.com/green/2022/11/02/meat-free-fridays-catholic-tradition-could-slash-global-carbon-emissions-study-finds

[153] Francis X. Weiser, Handbook of Christian Feasts and Customs (New York: Harcourt, 1958), p. 156 – 157.

[154] Rev. F.B. Jamison, "Catechism of Perseverance," Translated from the French of Monsignor Gaume, (James Duffy, 1866), p. 380.

[155] Dom Guéranger, *The Liturgical Year: Lent* (Burns & Oates, 1912), p. 34 – 35.

[156] Accessed via http://www.stsophiaukrainian.cc/resources/thefastingseasons/

[157] Adam Hoffman, "Does Dieting Actually Make Your Stomach Shrink?," Accessed via https://www.smithsonianmag.com/science-nature/does-dieting-actually-make-your-stomach-shrink-180955521/

[158] Rev. Athanasius Iskander, "Practical Spirituality According to the Desert Fathers," (St Shenouda Press, 2011).

[159] A Homily of St. Bede the Venerable taken from Book 3, Ch. 38, on Mark Chapter 9 as quoted in the 1962 Roman Breviary published in English and Latin by Baronius Press in 2017, p. 1154.

[160] Rev. Dominic M. Prümmer, *Handbook of Moral Theology* (The Mercier Press, Limited, 1949), p. 224.

[161] Accessed via https://archive.org/details/parishguidestmar00slsnuoft

[162] While much of the Eastern Churches have adopted the watered down fasting in the Latin Rite, the traditional Eastern fasting schedule can give us additional inspiration for how to incorporate ancient periods of fasting in our own lives. See the traditional fasting in place for the Eastern Catholics as of 1922 at http://holyunia.blogspot.com/2010/08/traditional-byzantine-rite-fast-and.html.

[163] Father Lawrence Lew, "Rekindling the Embers, (New Liturgical Movement, 2012).

[164] St. Basil the Great, *Homilia De Jejunio II*, § 4, ed. Gaume, tom. ii, p. 17.

[165] Henry Robert Percival, *The Seven Ecumenical Councils of the Undivided Church* (Parker, 1900), p. 461.

[166] St. Thomas Aquinas, Summa Theologiae III, Q. 80, a. 8, reply to objection 3, Accessed via https://www.newadvent.org/summa/4080.htm

[167] St. Augustine, Letter 54, Accessed via http://www.newadvent.org/fathers/1102054.htm.

[168] Gerhard Rauschen, *Eucharist and Penance in the First Six Centuries of the Church* (B. Herder, 1913), p. 150.

[169] Henry Robert Percival, *The Seven Ecumenical Councils of the Undivided Church* (Parker, 1900), p 378.

[170] Rev. Herbert Thurston SJ, *American Ecclesiastical Review* (Catholic University of America Press, 1934), vol. 91, p. 577.

[171] St. Thomas Aquinas, Summa Theologiae III, Q. 80, a. 8, reply to objection 1, Accessed via https://www.newadvent.org/summa/4080.htm

[171] St. Augustine, Letter 54, Accessed via http://www.newadvent.org/fathers/1102054.htm.

[172] James Morton, *Byzantine Religious Law in Medieval Italy* (OUP Oxford, 2021), p. 17 – 22.

[173] *The Pedalion*, trans. Denver Cummings, J Masterjohn, ed. (The Orthodox Christian Educational Society, 2005), p. 711.

[174] St. Thomas Aquinas, Summa Theologiae III, Q. 80, a. 8, reply to objection 5, Accessed via https://www.newadvent.org/summa/4080.htm

[175] St. Thomas Aquinas, Summa Theologiae III, Q. 80, a. 8, reply to objection 4, Accessed via https://www.newadvent.org/summa/4080.htm

[176] Denzinger 626 taken from *The Sources of Catholic Dogma* (Preserving Christian Publications, 2020), p. 211.

[177] *Catechism of the Council of Trent for Parish Priests* (Joseph F. Wagner, 1947), p. 248.

[178] Patrick Morrisroe. "Holy Communion." The Catholic Encyclopedia. Vol. 7. (Robert Appleton Company, 1910), Accessed via http://www.newadvent.org/cathen/07402a.htm.

[179] Stanislaus Woywod, *The New Canon Law: A Commentary and Summary of the New Code of Canon Law* (Joseph F Wagner, 1918), p. 172.

[180] Rev. Dominic M. Prümmer, *Handbook of Moral Theology* (The Mercier Press, Limited, 1949), p. 270 – 271.

[181] Ibid.

[182] Ibid.

[183] Rev. Windfrid Herbst, *Questions of Catholics Answers* (1946), p. 82.

[184] Ibid., p. 82 – 83.

[185] Pope Pius XII, *Christus Dominus: Concerning the Discipline to be Observed with Respect to the Eucharistic Fast* (January 6, 1953).

[186] Pope Pius XII, *Sacram Communionem: On Laws of Fasting and the Evening Mass* (March 25, 1957).

[187] Tertullian, *De Corona*, Accessed via https://www.newadvent.org/fathers/0304.htm.

[188] Archdale A. King, *Liturgies of the Religious Orders* (The Bruce Publishing Company, 1955), p. 6.

[189] Rev. Shawn Turnick, *Evening Masses and Days of Obligation Historical Development and Modern Norms*, (Thesis, The Catholic University of America, 2016), Accessed via https://archive.ccwatershed.org/media/pdfs/17/11/25/19-25-37_0.pdf.

[190] Ibid.

[191] St. Pius X, Decree on Frequent Communion, Dec. 20, 1905, art. 4.

[192] The Roman Ritual, Part I, Accessed via https://www.ewtn.com/catholicism/library/roman-ritual-part-i-11882

[193] Pope Pius XII, "Mediator Dei," Accessed via https://www.papalencyclicals.net/pius12/p12media.htm

[194] Ibid.

[195] St. John Chrysostom, Homily 27 on First Corinthians, "Nicene and Post-Nicene Fathers, First Series, Vol. 12," Edited by Philip Schaff. Translated by Talbot W. Chambers, (Christian Literature Publishing Co.,

1889). Revised and edited for New Advent by Kevin Knight. Accessed via http://www.newadvent.org/fathers/220127.htm

[196] The Responses of Pope Nicholas I to the Questions of the Bulgars A.D. 866 (Letter 99). Translated by W. L. North from the edition of Ernest Perels, in MGH Epistolae VI, Berlin, 1925, pp.568-600. Accessed via https://sourcebooks.fordham.edu/basis/866nicholas-bulgar.asp

[197] 1983 Code of Canon Law, Canon 1174.2

[198] Rev. Heribert Jone, "Moral Theology: Englished and Adapted to the Laws and Customs of the United States of America," (Newman Press, 2009), p. 285.

[199] Rev. Edward Quigley, "The Divine Office A Study of the Roman Breviary," (Good Press, 2009), p. 81.

[200] Rev. Thomas Crean, "The Mass and the Saints", (Ignatius Press, 2009).

[201] St. Thomas Aquinas, Summa Theologiae III, Q. 83, a. 2, Accessed via https://www.newadvent.org/summa/4083.htm

[202] St. Thomas Aquinas, Summa Theologiae III, Q. 83, a. 2, reply to objection 3, Accessed via https://www.newadvent.org/summa/4083.htm

[203] Rev. Herbert Jone, *op cit.*, p. 358.

[204] Pope Pius XII, *Sacram Communionem: On Laws of Fasting and the Evening Mass* (March 25, 1957).

[205] Translation of Lesson 4 from the Divine Office Hour of Matins on December 6th, Accessed via https://isidore.co/divinum/cgi-bin/horas/Pofficium.pl?date1=12-06-2016

[206] Dom Guéranger, *The Liturgical Year: Time after Pentecost: Volume 2* (Burns & Oates, 1909), p. 390.

[207] "Flesh meat" is defined as all meats other than fish and seafood.

[208] Fr. Hardon defines a *frustulum* as "The small portion of food, a few ounces, formerly permitted at breakfast on fast days. This was provided by canon law (Canon 1251), which permitted taking some food, morning and evening, in addition to the one full meal per day." A collation is "A light meal that is allowed in addition to a full meal on fasting days." A frustulum is 2 ounces and a collation is generally understood to be up to 8 ounces.

Made in the USA
Las Vegas, NV
26 November 2024

12687124R00108